Conscious Adulting

In the Digital Age

Melissa Baker (Honey Bee)

ISBN: 979-8-9866587-0-4

To my grandparents, for their insights and thousands of questions.

To my younger self & all the young adults growing wiser in the digital age.

Table of Contents

Introduction

"The ultimate freedom is a free mind, and we need technology on our team to help us live, feel, think and act freely." —Tristan Harris (2016)

It was a Sunday morning. I woke up early to start my day in silence. My phone alarm rang from across the house, a beautiful song with the lyrics, "I feel peace near / I am safe here." I went to turn it off and get ready for sadhana, a daily spiritual practice, something I've developed over the past six years. My intention is to do it for thirty to sixty minutes. It occasionally gets cut short with my child coming in and asking for breakfast, the dog begging for my attention, or even my mind's effective strategy of making something feel more urgent than connecting with this inner wisdom. On this morning, I practiced a Kriya, or set of postures, from Kundalini yoga, which I was teaching later that morning at a dear friend's tea shop.

As a digital wellness and yoga teacher, I can best prepare by engaging in a spiritual practice myself. On this day, I showed up to teach the class with my flute, a well-prepared playlist, my mat, and paper for the students to explore their own creativity when the class was complete. By the end of the class, people cried, smiled, and trusted in their creative and spiritual processes. As I was packing up my things, I observed one student turn their phone back on.

As she waited for it to come back to life, I smiled and said, "I appreciate you turning off your phone during class! It's nice to disconnect, even if it is for an hour."

"Yeah, I need to do it. Unplug to plug back in."

It took me a few seconds to understand what she was saying, and when I had that "Ah-ha" moment, I savored her words. "Unplug to plug back in." Plug back into herself, her creativity, spiritual practice, body, thoughts, and life. I replied with excitement. "I've been writing a book about this for about five years." I laughed.

"Is the reason why it isn't published because of this thing?" She shook her phone as it lit up, capturing the attention of the naturally lit room.

I laughed. "Partly, yes! There are too many opportunities for it to take my attention." In reality, it was much more than the device. All the tabs open on my computer, the four jobs I worked, the relationship I started, the child I had, the phone that buzzed and buzzed and buzzed.

The tea shop owner chimed in, "I usually turn my phone off for one or two days a week." After a few more minutes of energizing conversation about our device habits and boundaries, we ended the conversation positively. We concluded that taking breaks from our devices, even for an hour, can be helpful, if unnecessary, for a high quality of life.

Plugged In

In my sophomore year of college studying health education and behavior, I noticed the excessive use of our devices.

Over the years, research has supported my own realizations as a millennial living in the digital age. At the ripe age of twenty-two, I discovered digital wellness before it was a "thing."

According to the Digital Wellness Institute, digital wellness "is a way of life, while using technology, that promotes optimal health and well-being." An individual integrates "body, mind, and Spirit to live more fully within the human, natural, and digital communities" (Blankson and Hersher 2021). I thought I was crazy, being the only one on the bus without headphones in my ears—plugged in. I'd walk around campus and count how many people were looking down at their phones down the path—plugged in. As a child, I was around my parents who plugged into the constant noise of the TV, news, and radio.

But what does plugging in honestly look like as an adult? Like Tristan Harris's quote at the beginning of this section, "The ultimate freedom is a free mind, and we need technology that's on our team to help us live, feel, think and act freely" (2016). Do we free our minds by giving our devices all the power to capture our attention? Or do we free our minds by plugging into something higher than ourselves and living with purpose instead of being a victim of what the phone wants us to be attentive toward? What exactly are you plugging yourself into daily? A spiritual practice or Instagram? Is it getting outside and connecting with nature? Is it waking up before the sun rises and chanting a mantra, or sound vibration, or doing something that makes your heart fill with love?

This book solves an overdue, multidimensional problem of recognizing and confronting our digital habits. I was never taught to use technology consciously. Technology was next to me when I slept. Its bright light woke me up in the morning instead of the sun. Texts and news articles concluded my day, and I often slept restlessly at night. It affected my relationships with friends and family. Trying to have a conversation with someone who has their iPad on their lap, the TV running, and their phone sitting next to them is a battle that tech wins over others' voices.

Like many, I was born into this brilliant time of constant stimulation from cell phones, TVs, iPads, computers, screens, and the newest devices to supposedly enhance the lives of humanity. Tech companies promised a better tomorrow for our children, though the creators themselves didn't allow their children to have smartphones until their late teens. Some estimates show that US adults now spend roughly seven hours on a screen each day (Moody 2022). With phones, thirty-one percent of adults report they are almost constantly online (Perrin and Atske 2021). Where do we go from here? What is the magic pill I can take to help me feel connected to nature, myself, others around me, and my purpose on this earth?

The magic "pill" is not to avoid technology or shame it for existing. If this were a book about how to avoid screens, it would be short:

Go out in the woods, without your phone, Apple Watch, iPad, laptop, and other beeping, buzzing, vibrating, talking machines, and stay out there for the rest of your life. Oh, and if you see anyone using such devices, avoid them because they might be a robot. The end.

As you might imagine, we wouldn't get deep into the woods without being hit by anxiety from detaching from these devices. What about using our GPS, step counter, or YouTube to tell us how to pitch the tent? Screens have their place in the world, and it is your choice to empower yourself to be different in how you approach them. It is time for you to act consciously with your devices, using them with awareness, intention, and a deeper connection to your purpose. Now is the time to accept digital wellness as an indicative part of becoming an adult. "Adulting," defined by Oxford Learner's Dictionaries, is "the practice of behaving in a way characteristic of a responsible adult, especially the accomplishment of mundane but necessary tasks" (2022).

Conscious Adulting uses awareness, willpower, intuition, and optimal habits so we live in alignment with our True Selves while learning to navigate in-person and online spaces. You can be twenty-two or sixty-five; it doesn't matter. You can always "opt-in" to improve your relationship with screens.

Conscious Adulting looks honestly at all parts of you and your relationship to your inner and outer screens in the world you grew up in and your current reality. On our inner screen, a movie is constantly playing. It is the movie of your thoughts, past experiences, future expectations, emotions, and bodily sensations. Constantly, your awareness is watching what is on your inner screen. This witness is your consciousness, and with techniques like yoga and meditation, you will become less reactive to what you notice on your inner screen and more aware of this conscious awareness that is observing. I refer to this consciousness throughout the book as awareness, Spirit, Soul, or Universe. Some refer to this as God, Atma, or Christ.

It's a guide to assure you that you are not alone in this adjustment of integrating technology consciously into your everyday life. Once we establish a base for exploring this healthy relationship with inner and outer technology, we dive into owning who you are and expressing that through various mediums.

We discuss digital wellness and behavior nearly as little as we address postpartum with pregnancy. Before I had my first child, many mothers I spoke with mentioned all the beautiful things about birth and having a newborn but rarely was there mention of the loneliness, physical pain, and hormonal shifts that occur. After I gave birth, I thought to myself, *why don't more people speak about this darkness that is just as real as all the beauty that comes after a child?* At the same time, I felt like a warrior for giving birth to a human and felt my ego get in the way of me reaching out for help. Digital wellness is one of those topics we may be too afraid or prideful to discuss because "we think we know it all."

We weren't born asking for a relationship with a foreign object that is not human. It is one of those mysteries discovered if you dive deep into the hands of personal experience and accurate sources of information. Throughout this book, I will talk about my personal experiences with the "digital postpartum," or the aftermath of a human born into a world where digital life is almost as important as real life. Where do they come together, and where do they differ for you? I invite you to question your relationship with digital well-being and other areas of your life, including physical, mental, emotional, social, and spiritual health. And not just the feel-good stuff but the parts where you struggle, where if you didn't get in your own way, you'd reach out for help and seek answers, not from Google, to what you are experiencing.

Where You Are

———————

We are all at different levels of understanding technology, depending on our upbringing. Regardless of where you come from, Conscious Adulting sheds light on your authentic voice and how to use that in digital and human interactions. Everyone learns how to find this voice differently. Through small yet impactful moments of being a mother, a business owner, a teacher, a trusting friend, and a forgiving sister, I strengthened my voice. Through this path, I have become a certified digital wellness educator, certified health education specialist, certified Kundalini, Hatha/Vinyasa, kids yoga teacher, group fitness teacher, and certified mother. I am joking on that last one, but anyone who has had a child may agree that having one of those beautiful souls is like a certified rite of passage to another world.

Every week, I taught an aqua class called "ENERGY H2O" to an older population, with the occasional pregnant woman. One sweet seventy-something lady drives forty-five minutes in her Volkswagen Beetle every week to attend.

One Monday afternoon after class, she swam over to the pool's edge where I was standing. She said in her German accent, "Thank you so much, Melissa. I love your class because I don't do cardio often, if at all, and I feel like I get cardio in your class, but it's gentle and fun. All the other teachers I have taken. . ." She paused and threw her arms up, splashing water in every direction. She raised her voice, "GO, GO, PUSH HARDER!" Her voice echoed throughout the pool area, and I couldn't help but laugh at this sweet woman impersonating those kickass teachers. "You motivate us differently and make us work at the level we are."

I've heard this compliment echo through the decade I have been a teacher. These stories, teachings, and practical techniques transparently shared in this book are here to meet you where you are. They may challenge your habits and beliefs, but I assure you they will not yell, "GO, GO, PUSH HARDER!" May these words feel like water. Though you can flow with water, there may be some resistance you will feel, like the sting of cool raindrops pricking your skin. After the storm, there is that feeling of cleansing, rejuvenating life. There is a sparkle and growth in the garden of our hearts. We have so much to learn from digital wellness, and it has a lot to learn from us.

Our relationships with technology can be symbiotic if we acknowledge its addictive nature and use it in a way that serves us. For example, I have an app called FOCUS that blocks my social media news feed and instead provides a positive quote. "There is only one success—to be able to spend your life in your own way" by Christopher Morley was the quote I received the other day (2020).

There can be a cooperative exchange between us and tech to enhance the quality of our lives. In the same way, there is a dance between giving and receiving in a partnership or relationship with ourselves. Digital wellness helps us open to this channel of collaboration with your digital devices so it is serving and empowering you to be your authentic self.

Expectations

Before opening the pages of any book, I always wonder about the format and how the writer will share what they want me to hear. The book is organized to allow readers to read and complete exercises in the order that works best for them. The first sections of each chapter are based on my personal experiences, with wisdom and lessons I have learned that may reflect your own experiences. It is in these sections where I hope you say, "Ah, I am not alone in this. There is a way."

The second part of each chapter consists of Tech Steps. Tech Steps are created for you to dive into your inner environment and examine the relationships between your inner and outer screens and the people around you. This journaling portion can be written in a separate journal or in the pages at the back of this book. These crucial exercises apply what you are learning. Knowledge does not equal behavior. However, taking small, actionable steps creates internal and external change.

Tech Steps help you get to the root of your behaviors concerning screens. They will allow you access to your inner guidance to live with more consciousness and protection around your energy and attention. You will find that chapter one goes with Tech Step 1 and so on. You can read sections one and two separately or together. Whichever method you choose, I gently encourage you to read both sections to gain the most out of your time and energy. They are the yin and the yang. The first section is the yin, the energy of passiveness, and the second section is the yang, the point of action. Both work together to create the whole experience of Conscious Adulting.

Chapter One

Escape

I'm bored. I'm going to veg out and watch shows all day," I said to my freshman college roommate, Andie, early Saturday morning as she played on her phone in her pajamas on the couch. It was around nine in the morning, and I had already been up for an hour deciding what I would do that day. I'd gotten most of my schoolwork done. It was drizzling outside, which was typical for fall time, or any time, in Florida. I was bored and programmed to believe one of the few solutions for alleviating that feeling was technology. I grabbed my phone to pull up Facebook, scrolling through things that only took me further away from what may fulfill me. Out of jealousy and envy, I posted a photo of my friends and me from last week. The photo was taken at the best part of our night. The picture didn't capture another friend crying over her boyfriend and me asleep on the couch by 10:30 p.m.

That morning represented many mornings in my last years of high school and first years of college. The outer screens surrounding me since I was a child distracted and dissatisfied me. First, it was TV, then the flip phone, and after, a touchscreen phone with various apps to steal my precious and innocent attention. Technology was integrated into my life from the start of my very existence, and as humans do, I adapted. Maybe your journey began with beepers, video games, or your parent's phone.

I remember when the TV or phone wasn't connected to me like a second brain. After my elementary school days, I'd bike around the neighborhood, knocking at the doors of kids around my age. "Hey, Mrs. Porter, can Kelsey come out and play?" Her mom would smile and give her the okay to join me. I'd run back to my bike and ride in circles, daydreaming about what games we'd play until she came out. Experiences of boredom led to ideas, dreams, and expansive imaginary thoughts.

As children, my peers and I unknowingly started the habit of using screens, limiting exploration. As a result, I eventually addressed boredom with devices instead of my imagination. I'd sit in front of the TV on a Saturday morning. I'd lounge there for hours, unaware of my body's signals to move or eat because I wasn't taught how to tune into my body's wisdom and ask what it really needed.

Consequently, I'd get up, get a bowl of sugary cereal or whatever I could find to quiet down that small inner voice nudging me to get up and do something else. That inner voice was noticed occasionally while guiding me outside, kayaking down the river with my parents, or traveling to the beach with friends. Those moments brought me back to myself and rested my heart on what was true to life. When I look back on my childhood, I remember those times over the ones looking down at that tiny screen.

Like many people who grew up with emerging technology, my parents had no guidebook on how to use it. My generation was born into a situation where no one knew how this constant stimulation impacted our minds, bodies, and spirits. As I grew further from my inner voice and put my faith in the outside screens, it left me feeling empty and out of touch. The innocent child riding her bike was now sitting on the couch, spoon-fed "reality" TV and social media filters. This wasn't who I was, and I knew there was another way.

Breaking Free

When I was a physical education teacher, I'd ask the kids in my classes different questions to spark interest in being physical outside. "What are you going to do tonight when you get home? Will it be active?"

"Play video games! That's active, right?" one middle-schooler yelled sarcastically and got a chuckle out of a few other kids.

"Watch YouTube," another kid mumbled, ignoring the "active" part of the question.

These are the same children who came to class tired, scared of being outside because of bugs, and complaining about walking one lap, even after being inside the classroom most of the day. I did my best to express to them the importance of physical activity and being outside. It stuck for a few of them, while for others, it went right over their heads and into space, like the rest of the things they learned that day. I brought them on mindful walks, taught them yoga, and walked with the last kid who needed extra encouragement during mile day. But did it matter when they went home and consumed processed foods and violent video games? And what were their parents teaching them by their own behaviors? I tried not to judge, and I had much compassion for them, for I did the same thing when I was their age.

Sugar and television were my numbing creams of choice as a child. They were ways for me to not deal with my emotions, check out of life's obstacles, and check in to a world that felt like an escape. This habit remained with me throughout high school and college. The technology advanced to Netflix, Hulu, YouTube, or other live-streaming services, and the ice cream became non-dairy.

Years went by, and I was in college living with roommates, where I had complete freedom to direct my boredom. Sometimes, I entertained myself with a screen. Other times, I embraced my love for movement and exercise— which is why I was a physical education teacher for a few years. I'm one of those rare people who love to sweat and push myself a little past my comfort zone, and it made me feel freakin' amazing. Whether it was tennis, the gym, or running, exercising was a way to process and look at life differently. Some may find this creativity when going for a walk or using technology to get inspired by listening to a TED Talk or a favorite song. We all have ways of hiding from our inner and outer worlds, and we have methods for exploring them.

Professor Cal Newport (2016) wrote a book titled *Deep Work: Rules for Focused Success in a Distracted World*, where he distinguished two key terms to help us understand how we are focused. "Shallow work," defined as "non-cognitive, logistical," or minor duties performed in a state of distraction, and "deep work," which he describes as "professional activities performed in a state of distraction-free concentration that push your cognitive capabilities to their limit. These efforts create new value, improve your skill, and are hard to replicate" (Newport 2016). Most people, and many students, spend most of their time on shallow, low-value work. It is an easy option, including social media and video games. Our upbringing can affect our attention and our ability to shift into these deep states of work and play.

The brilliant thing about our brains is we can relearn how to focus and rewire our attention. You can experience deep work and explore that childlike boredom you may have missed out on by dissolving into a virtual world. The beautiful reality is right in front of you and within you.

A Yogic Twist Can Transform

On a Sunday afternoon under the Florida sun, which some people would call torture, I went on a run. I was tired of staring at my computer doing my last semester of college coursework. As I was running, I felt the endorphins pumping under my skin, and I thought about the cycle of life from a yogic perspective—the process of birth, life, death, and rebirth. I reflected on the habit I created, that might even be considered an addiction, of watching Netflix. As I ran up one of the most demanding hills in the neighborhood (yes, Florida does have some hills), I realized these habits can die and be reborn into something even more powerful. The energy I expended taking in these shows could be transformed into something more meaningful. If I was a filmmaker, or the shows inspired me, they might have meaning. But many of them consumed my thoughts, affected my sleep, and created unhealthy habits that did not serve me.

As sweat dripped into my eyes, some tears dripped out. I decided I was done numbing by watching pointless shows, and I was ready to confront all those emotions I hadn't dealt with for years and dive into myself without fear of what I would find, fully honoring it. When I got home from my run and self-pep talk, something in me shifted. I analyzed myself with less of a critical eye and more of a compassionate inner gaze. I called myself home from this detour from my true purpose, where I did harmful things to my body and mind, which affected my sleep, relationships, and love for myself. After years of looking away from this pain, I could confront and elevate it. I began examining beliefs lodged down below the surface of my everyday thoughts. The craving to escape was replaced with the fulfillment of growth. Though I opened up to those days, when I vegged out and watched shows one rainy day, I forgave myself for ignoring the quiet inner voice of what I truly needed. Ah, sweet forgiveness—my body and heart melted when I opened to that space.

In moments like that, when I had this "inner waking up," I didn't altogether remove technology, as it is nearly impossible to do that in today's digital age. I still enjoy watching a show with my partner or sharing some ice cream with friends once in a while. Sitting in front of the TV or my phone to escape became less of a nightly, naughty habit and transformed into a part of my life that I had more willpower over.

We can't blame screens for controlling us, even though a significant driver of technology companies is to grab and hold our attention. What is in our control is the force that drives the behavior. It is the root cause instead of the proximate cause. After I ran into this inner voice of wisdom when running that day, I jotted down my grand plan to heal and worked on transforming my screen habits. It took years, and there are certainly times when I forget and remember again. I discovered many of these habits formed during childhood, like eating dinner with my family every night while watching the news. Or standing side by side with friends, with all of us on our phones, not talking to each other. These social norms were not considered and disconnected me from this True Self, this inner voice, while I relied on my devices to instantaneously gratify me.

We can look into these experiences and emotions tied to our current behaviors to relearn what it means to connect to a deeper part of ourselves. Eventually, it sticks, not with ease and grace but with sacred rage, shame, and resentment. While breaking this self-sabotaging habit, these emotions passed through me, but I didn't push them down with a screen or sugar. When the urge to numb kept coming up, and coming up, and coming up again, I'd sit with it. I gave myself the time to feel. I would breathe, go outside, or talk to a friend, and finally, I listened to that subtle voice I call my True Self. There were times, though, I replaced the patterns inhibiting my growth with other excessive patterns, including marijuana and diet control. Over time, I realized this wouldn't be a simple fix. There was no "heal me" pill I could pop, and "poof!" all the emotional weight and heaviness would be healed. I didn't have a ton of money to spend on massages, acupuncture, and therapy. But I had incredibly supportive people around me, an environment that helped me foster this change, and a growing spiritual practice.

Some people on the spiritual path can use spirituality as an escape, just like a screen. When they don't want to deal with something, they sit alone and meditate for three hours. The spiritual ego can get in the way and make you believe you are higher or better than any life problem. Don't let it fool you. If you think you are super-spiritual, and that's the identity you are creating, take a second look at yourself and weed out what is an illusion to you. Just like our technology can be an escape, so can the illusion of spirituality, especially in the billion-dollar yoga pants and health supplements industry.

When this awareness of your inner truth is illuminated, any escape can be reborn into a conscious attitude of attention to the devices surrounding you and a lesson to tune into your inner wisdom. A beautiful journey occurs when we open up to what is holding us back, forgive, and transform. I see you doing the deep work.

Tech Step 1: Learn and Unlearn

Repeat after me: I agree to honesty and authenticity when journaling about my connection with screens.

Many habits we have learned concerning screens come from childhood and our early years of watching the people around us use screens. Such habits aren't good or bad, but they shape how we interact with ourselves and others. If your mother put down her phone when she spoke with you, you may have felt more seen, heard, and understood by her. If your father drank three or four beers while watching sports as soon as he got home and didn't pay attention to you during those times, you might have cultivated a different relationship with him, and the masculine in general. In other instances, as a child, sometimes we make up stories that genuinely don't make sense, and there doesn't need to be an explanation, but only a processing of the emotion to release it.

Start this Tech Step with free-flow writing about your childhood and how screens were integrated. What habits did your parents exemplify? What about your siblings or other people around you?

Choose a habit you have now concerning screens. Is it your excessive social media checks? Are you binge-watching shows on Netflix? Do you have obsessive thoughts about when he will text you back? Choose one. Just one. What areas of your life is this currently affecting (physical, mental, emotional, spiritual, environmental, professional, relational, or perhaps, none)?

Now, imagine you are having a conversation with that younger you. See yourself ten or twenty years younger, an innocent child who simply wants to feel loved, safe, and have a sense of belonging. Explain to that version of you in simple terms about technology. What would you tell this child? How would you explain to them what it is like to use screens with awareness? How would you share with them about this one tech habit that is pervading areas of your life currently? This conversation doesn't have to be written down. Like I was running during an awakening to screens, you can do this as you go on a run or walk outside. Talk to your younger self. Comfort yourself. Help yourself understand this habit.

Now do this with one or two more technology habits that positively or negatively affect your life.

Chapter Two

Overcome Illusions to Celebrate Reality

If you are thirty-five years old or younger, you have likely done one of the following in your existence on planet Earth:

You go to a friend's house to "talk" or "hang out" and spend most of your time on your phones or playing video games.

You sit at the dinner table with your family, the ones you love. Your phone is on your lap or in your pocket, and you're waiting for a coworker or friend to text you. You're eating, but it's all you're thinking about as your phone sits on your lap.

You watch TV while you eat a meal.

You take pictures of yourself and your partner, and when you look back at them, all you can see are your flaws.

You wake up in the morning tired because you were up late on your phone, watching a show or movie. Despite this tiredness, you start your day doing the same thing with a phone or iPad.

Throughout your day, you keep your phone in sight and check it almost every five minutes.

These are some habits that shape your relationship with technology. These are the small habits and behaviors that carry your relationship with yourself. Our daily actions contribute to our emotional, mental, social, digital, spiritual, occupational, and environmental well-being. Looking back, what are the moments you remember most?

When I was sixteen, I went to my first prom. A guy in the grade above me invited me to be his date. I went with him, thinking I was hot shit to go to prom with a guy one year older than me. I dressed up in a beautiful blue-and-white dress that reminded me of my favorite place, the ocean. I did my hair and makeup and posed for photos that made me look like I could have been famous. People made a huge deal of proms, especially online. The days after, I saw the photos go up on Facebook, including the ones I took. The moments of jealousy when he danced with another girl or the after-party filled with underage drinking and regretful decisions didn't appear online. Who gets a party bus with stripper poles for a high school prom and thinks nothing will happen?

Online, I weaved the life I wanted people to believe, mainly posting happy and celebratory times. I shaped my online identity from prom and high school highlight photos. Social media was an outlet to celebrate parts of my life, and it also took me away from other aspects of my life I didn't want to examine. I believed people to be a certain way based on how they acted on their online platform. Social media connected me and also trapped me. It expanded me. It contracted me. It opened me to information that a sixteen-year-old is probably better off not knowing. Social media hunched me over and closed me off to the data coming in from reality. Social media was deemed safe for my teenage self, even though depression and suicide rates have increased across the US in the past ten years, particularly among America's youth. This rise is attributed to the connection with technology and social platforms.

There was no conscious choice where I said to myself, "I will be a teenager who spends hours on a screen and cares more about my social media presence than my actual presence." I was labeled a "millennial," got in trouble for using my phone in class, and received calls from my grandpa when, bless his soul, he needed help changing his profile photo on Facebook. In high school and the first years of college, I knew technology better than I knew myself. I got over fifty likes on those prom-day photos and comments, which contributed to my self-worth. From my digital life, I found the superficial approval I sought. There was no looking within myself for that approval, because I did not feel emotionally secure.

According to The Center for Generational Kinetics, an Austin, Texas-based research firm, 42 percent of Gen Z—the people born in the mid to late 1990s to 2010s—more than any other generation, said social media affects how other people see you (Mastroianni 2016). The same percentage of Gen Z also said social media directly impacts how they feel about themselves. After graduating from high school and college and reprogramming this habit of looking outside myself, social media is no longer a part of my self-worth. I use it to inspire others and rarely spend time mindlessly scrolling. Yes, I still celebrate my life online, but the difference is I am present in the moment as it is happening. Then, once I post the moment, there isn't an obsession about who liked it and if I was good enough. And no one is perfect, so when I get trapped in the social comparison game, I notice my anxiety increases, my mind becomes scattered, and unhealthy thoughts enter my brain.

"I'm not good enough."

"I'm lonely."

"I want that life, not the one I'm living now."

Life is asking us to show up, not only on social media but for the moments that make up the collage of our story. Each and every day, celebrate where you are because this right now is what matters, not how many likes you get on your prom photos. What story are you feeding by engaging in social media? What stories are holding you back from growing personally, professionally, and spiritually?

Phoneliness

Is heart disease the number one killer in America? Or is it loneliness? The pandemic has influenced this epidemic of loneliness in America. A recent study from Harvard suggests that 61 percent of young adults and 35 percent of all Americans feel "seriously lonely" (Weissbourd et al. 2021). That same article quotes, "As a society, we do little to support emerging adults at precisely the time when they are dealing with the most defining, stressful decisions of their lives related to work, love, and identity. Who to love? What to do?" (Weissbourd et al. 2021).

It is evident that becoming an adult is hard enough, and with the use of social media, does it make it harder or easier? We can't blame all this on social media. However, we can look at how social media contributes to it. Has there been a time when you have felt isolated or lonely, and you went on social media instead of calling or texting a friend? You are not the only one. Worldwide, 420 million are estimated to suffer from internet and social media dependency (Cheng and Yee-lam Li 2014).

Even one of the most-followed people on the planet Selena Gomez has not been on the internet since 2018. She mentioned on Good Morning America, "I am happier, I am more present, I connect with more people. It makes me feel normal," (Dailey 2022).

Even mental health therapists and entrepreneurs experience feelings of being too connected to their phones.

A friend of mine, a mental health therapist and a millennial, explained to me one day about her relationship with social media and her digital devices. As a child, Raf didn't grow up with a TV and still doesn't have one in her house. Even though she doesn't own a TV, she feels like she has a small TV in her hand all the time. When I asked whether her relationship with screens was healthy, she said yes at first. Then, we got a little deeper. "If I'm being honest with myself, I don't like to look at my screen time because it feels embarrassing because I have this precious life, but I'm looking at a screen all day long. How often has my cat wanted me to pet her, and I was busy looking at a TikTok," she expressed.

Raf always has her phone on her, although one grad school course changed her relationship with social media.

As an addiction course assignment, she had to give something up for three months to help see how it would feel for someone in sobriety. She chose social media and, as a result, felt more connected to the people in her life. Years later, she only has Instagram and TikTok accounts. Raf doesn't share a lot, but she consumes for hours because of the individualized content curation. She believes that who she follows inspires her unless it is a cute couple that makes her jealous.

Social media can be beneficial and support your, depending on how you use it. Because Raf listened to people talk all day for her profession, social media is a way for her to unwind. She also uses it to connect with people she already connects with in real life. It is essential to note our social media use affects our well-being, and it can go both ways. It can enhance our life, relationships, and the way we care for ourselves, create feelings of loneliness, decrease our connection, and influence our mental health. So what is authentic, and what is an illusion?

Melissa Baker (Honey Bee)

Maya

In Vedic Yogic traditions, the term "maya" means "that which is not." Of course, social media and phones are not an illusion, as they may sit next to you, clearly there. However, maya comes into play when you superimpose a memory or experience on the current reality, creating something that isn't really there. According to Hinduism, under maya's influence, the Atman (the soul) mistakenly identifies with the body. If a person is illusioned to believe I am only a body, they may accept such thoughts as "I am white; I am my social media image," or "This is my house and religion." The illusioned soul identifies with the temporary body and everything connected, such as race, religion, gender, family, nation, bank balance, or a phone. The soul aspires to control and enjoy matter under this sense of false ego (false identity). However, a person under this illusion continuously serves lust, greed, and anger. This exhaustive cycle of maya continues until it is broken.

Are you a cycle breaker? My guess is yes. The illusion of social media has a place, yet it is your choice to become deeply aware of how and why you are using it. This process starts inside.

Everyone uses their devices differently, whether for work, play, connection, or all of the above. Our devices don't make it easy to disconnect, though sometimes it is crucial to improve our phoneliness. This phenomenon of phoneliness is a state where a person's social media use contributes to feelings of loneliness, which can, in turn, affect social media use. It is vital to get clear on using your social media so it doesn't use you. A study done in 2018 measured 143 undergraduates at the University of Pennsylvania who were randomly assigned to either limit Facebook, Instagram, or Snapchat use to ten minutes per platform per day or to use social media as usual for three weeks (Hunt et al. 2018). The group showed significant reductions in loneliness and depression over three weeks compared to the control group. Both groups showed significant decreases in anxiety and fear of missing out over baseline, suggesting a benefit of increased self-monitoring. This is one of the many studies that directly shows limiting social media can affect your health. I'm not offering any specific method, because you know what will work best for you, and if you don't know yet, you will after this next Tech Step.

Tech Step 2: Reality & Illusion

Social media has replaced so much human connection, except there is one issue: it isn't the natural or spiritual connection we are all seeking and craving in our lives. Since the pandemic, you may likely spend more time on social media than on actual in-person connections. Let's take a dive down the rabbit hole of your relationship to social media and human connection so you can decipher what is an illusion and what is real in your life.

James Roberts, PhD, a marketing professor at Baylor University's Hankamer School of Business, wrote the book *Too Much of a Good Thing: Are You Addicted to Your Smartphone?* He asks questions that can give you an idea of how addicted you might be to social media:

> **"Salience:** Is social media use heavily integrated into your daily routine?

Tolerance: Do you spend progressively more time on social media to get the same satisfaction?

Euphoria: Do you rely on social media as a source of excitement or cope with boredom or loneliness?

Withdrawal: Do you need to use social media and feel edgy or anxious when you cannot?

Relapse: Do attempts to quit or reduce social media use fail?

Conflict: Does social media cause problems in your life or disputes with loved ones?" (Roberts 2016).

Bonus: Practical Growth

Open the social media app you use the most. Scroll for a moment and take note of what you see. What type of posts do you end up liking? What posts seem to be the most popular?

Posts showing off something typically do the best online, whether that be someone's looks, car, or travels.

Before you like something on social media, do you ever ask yourself how real a post is?

One more for the road to what's real:

How do you view yourself through the lens of social media? Does that reflect who you truly are?

This identity you have created online starts at a young age, in those proms or awkward middle school days. Let these questions open a door to exploring your own creativity, your own True Self, and a deeper connection to that quiet voice calling your Spirit through the maya.

Chapter Three

Bambas & the Creative Call

I am about to sit down and write a story I have been thinking about for days. The story is about a conversation I had with my dad when I was fifteen. The other day, he told me how he vividly remembered picking me up from school and me saying to him in the car, while tears dripped down my face, "Mom never listens to me! I've been telling her to schedule an appointment with a back doctor for months because I think something is wrong with my back." After that car ride, the appointment was made, and on the day of the appointment, the doctor showed me a picture of a fifty-two spinal curvature. That same doctor also told me, "A significant scoliosis surgery is the best way to correct it."

Just as I remembered the details of this emotionally charged, life-changing story, my partner, Michael, walked through the door with bags of groceries. "Can you please take these to the kitchen?" he said sweetly and walked away to the car to grab a few more. My first thought was, "How could he? No, absolutely not. I am doing something important right now. This story will disappear if I don't write it." Then I took a few breaths and took responsibility for my emotional reaction. Instead of speaking up about what I was doing and how it was important to me, because of fear of how he would react, I reluctantly pouted to the kitchen like a ten-year-old to help him put away the groceries. My inner child and creative energy dimmed.

It was rare that I got a quiet moment to write with my entire focus. It was partly my fault because I usually had to clean the house, create my schedule for the week, review my schedule three or four times, feed my dog, make some tea, and then just when I'm about to sit down and write, my phone buzzes, or the man I love walks in with groceries, or a baby cries, or a call comes in, or something "more important" than my own creative process disturbs the words caged in my mind, waiting to be unleashed on the page. Did you know it takes twenty-five minutes on average to refocus on a task after an interruption?

I took the groceries to the kitchen and began to put them away out of habit. Then Michael came into the room and pointed out the Israeli peanut snack called "Bambas" filled with hazelnut, which he got at the store. He opened the bag and met my gaze with a look of heavenly satisfaction. "Oh wow," he chuckled, impressed with the flavor. I had to try one, or three, at that point, and I did. They were delicious. But I imagined a blank page waiting for my words in the other room.

Michael and I put all the food away, and he scoped out the kitchen before cooking a traditional Indian lunch with samosas, palak paneer, and coconut rice. He saw dishes from breakfast sitting in the sink and asked nicely if I could do them because he likes to cook in a clean kitchen. I took a deep breath, tilted my head back, and let out a childlike groan. "Fine," I remarked unenthusiastically. It took me less than two minutes, but Michael could tell something else was bothering me. He picked up the bag of Bambas and grabbed a few, waiting for me to share what was going on with my emotions. I took them from his hand and said, "You've been waiting all morning to cook, so cook." I spoke with the same childish attitude. This remark was only a reflection of my inner story that I have been waiting to write, so write!

"Melissa, what are you needing right now? I didn't say you had to do the dishes now." He genuinely wanted to know what I was experiencing. He knew I was about to start my moon cycle, so he trod lightly on my emotional water.

"Right before you came in the door, I was about to write something significant and creative, and then you told me to help with the groceries and now the dishes. What's next?" I felt frustrated with myself primarily for not voicing my boundaries and getting distracted as a result. I paused. "I am going back into my office to write what I need to write, and then I will come back out a much happier person." I gave him back the bag of Bambas and left the room to go back into my office. He grabbed a few out of the bag and watched me walk away into the spotless sanctuary that I spent the morning cleaning instead of writing. And now, here I am.

Michael, Bambas, groceries, and dishes are all things that are valuable and assets to my life, but they also have the potential to take me away from my creative process in the same way technology does. Distractions came long before our cellular devices were invariably woven into our messy world. Our phones can make the human mind feel like a squirrel. In the book *The Distracted Mind: Ancient Brains in a High-Tech World* by Adam Gazzaley and Larry Rosen (2016), it says, "We are like a squirrel with an attention disorder, constantly jumping from tree to tree, sampling a few tasty morsels, and leaving many more behind as he jumps to the next tree, and the next and the next. It sounds exhausting, and, as we have shown, it is negatively affecting our safety, relationships, school and job performance, and mental health."

The creative process is delicate and fills everybody's lives differently, even if you perceive yourself as not creative. Creativity comes in waves, and capturing an idea in the digital age is as easy as catching a fast, tiny fish with a small net. Have you ever been in a conversation saying something awkward or silly right when the room gets quiet? You hear your own voice and wake up to your own sound.

Whether it's writing, drawing, making jewelry, or playing music, you are tapping into a vulnerable part of yourself. That quiet Self is an energy that needs time to appear and unfold. It requires patience.

For most of my life, stimulants and noises that distract me from this creative process have crowded me. That awkward time of silence in a noisy room happened for me when I learned to meditate, practice yoga, and get quiet enough to use that energy and channel it into creating the things that moved me. The only way I could find silence to create was by standing up for my own boundaries and not letting other people or screens regulate my creative schedule, which comes and goes depending on the season. The phone controls my attention better than Michael and Bambas on an average day.

Our phone constantly buzzes and beeps for our attention like a whining puppy. It directs our attention to the screen outside instead of our own internal screen. There is a time and place for putting away groceries, just like there is a time and place for our phones. To regulate our creativity and the calling of our Spirit, we need a break from looking down at our phone or having it near us. We are not perfect, and occasionally our creative process will be interrupted. During those times, forgiveness and compassion are the places to tap into. After that day, Michael and I talked about blocks of time I could focus on my writing, which helped me be more intentional with my time.

Creating is a process that looks different for everyone, and setting limits is one way to direct your energy toward what you choose to do instead of what other people and things ask of you. I have no regrets about helping my partner whenever he needs help. At the same time, I own my time, energy, and where I choose to direct my attention. My story about a life-changing scoliosis surgery was birthed onto the page with that ownership.

The next time I sat down to write, it was very different. I had two hours at my treadmill desk. Michael had made me a cute sign that hung outside my home office door and read, "Do not disturb, Honey Bee is creatively and intentionally working." The first eleven minutes were dedicated to a breathing meditation to tap into my creativity and clear any mental blocks standing in my way. These first minutes may look like movement, inspiring TED talk, or journaling for others. It worked like a crystal. I felt radiant and in tune with the inner voice I had been searching for when I'd distract myself by cleaning the house or doing anything else but what my spirit was calling me toward. From that time forward, I made space for meditation in my day, whether to prepare for the day or go into a big meeting. Sometimes, my meditation consisted of a minute of silent prayer before work. I began to work past the blocks stopping me from writing and living my best Self. I owned what was blocking me and scattered sacredness throughout my day.

Tech Step 3: Tap into Your Creativity

Meditation is one of those experiences that is different for everyone.

There are a billion, maybe more, meditations, as well as numerous classes and apps to help you meditate—silent or loud, breath-focused or sound-focused, moving or still, morning or evening, energetic or soothing, even laughing or crying. Perhaps your meditation is in your creative practice like writing is for me.

Meditation and yoga are some of the highest practices you can do to help with . . . well, to say it bluntly, weeding out the BS and clearly seeing yourself. This process is a journey with no end, but which roots and expands you, calming you and releasing your power. It helps you remember and release. By breaking your inner beliefs, patterns, and distractions, you can piece them back together according to your higher purpose.

When you've created a meditation routine that works for you, whether you learn from the internet or in-person from a skilled teacher, you will feel those emotions and old stories you've been distracting yourself from. Like, really feel it all. You're not numb or seduced by fear and desire. You are standing firm in your own inner strength. You are awake. That sounds nice, huh?

The intention of this Tech Step is to implement methods for prioritizing creativity in your life. You will find yourself with increased clarity in decision-making, deeper focus, and higher energy.

Dedicate one to twenty minutes before you work on a project or creative task to sit with yourself or a group of people. Whatever it is, use this time and space to become aware and clear the obstacles in your way. I am not making this too specific or telling you all the things I do in my personal meditation practice because I invite you to explore what this looks like for you at this time in your life.

Answer the questions below:

What are your top five distractions from staying focused on your creative projects?

I can start with, 1. Phone

Write how you can prevent these distractions from getting in the way next time you create.

1. Put the phone out of sight for one hour.

Now, write a specific plan for the next time you decide to work on your creative project. Example: I will spend five minutes listening to my favorite inspirational song before I work. Or I will say this prayer, "Universe, guide my heart, body, mind, and Spirit to surrender to the story I am creating. May I feel inspired, focused, and open to the signs you choose to send me as I write." Feel the inspiration that follows. Place this plan on your desk or your creative space as a gentle reminder that this inner voice matters.

Chapter Four

Got Your Back

I will never forget that day. I never saw you cry so hard in my life," my dad, Bill, told me five years after life curved me in a different direction. To be exact, it was a fifty-two-degree curve in my spine. I remembered that day all too well.

"Mom never listens to me! I've been telling her to schedule me an appointment with a back doctor for months because I think something is wrong with my back." The little girl inside me reflected on those days when I'd be playing quietly behind my mother's desk while she worked on the computer. "Can you play with me?" I'd ask with innocence. "Sorry, sweetie. I'm working," she responded, still looking at her computer.

We got the appointment scheduled for that upcoming week. I received X-rays of my spine for the first time. The doctor came in with an iPad to explain, "This picture on the screen shows a severe spinal curvature, and you will need surgery if you don't want to be in pain the rest of your life." Immediately, my dad and I broke into tears, astonished. Devastated. As many shocked people would, I went home and immediately got on the internet to research the surgery. Some stories were terrible, and others made me have hope. Overall, I left the computer with my head spinning even more. The surgery was booked for three months away, days before the spring break of my sophomore year in high school.

The day before my surgery, I had a sleepover with one of my best friends, Emily. We stayed up late doing backbends, laughing, and cherishing the last moments I would have to channel my inner gymnast. At 5:00 a.m. the following day, we dropped Emily off early and drove to the hospital, where I underwent surgery to get titanium rods placed along my spine.

When I woke up in the post-anesthesia care unit next to my mom, I smiled. Grumpy and numb, I slid in and out of sleep. Though my memories are obscured by the haze of anesthesia, I recollect doctors coming and going, a catheter hooked to my side, and a line of black stitches woven down my spine. I took my first few painful steps with my dad and felt optimistic that I could recover and live my life. Four days later, my parents wheeled me out of the hospital to continue my recovery journey. Being so limited in what I could do was excruciating, humbling, embarrassing, and eye-opening.

I had a little desk on top of my bed where my laptop was set up for homeschool, a TV in front of my bed, and a walker and back brace to help me heal. Day by day, I worked with the body to restore my physical health. I kept listening to that inner voice of determination and positivity telling me I could do this. Even when my mom had to shower me, and I'd be frustrated and embarrassed that I couldn't do it myself, I look back with gratitude for my parents' sacrifices to care for me during that time.

After going through traumatic surgery at fifteen, I realized that the physical body is a magnificent gift many of us take for granted. I see people slouched over almost everywhere I go, consuming stimulating media, junk food, and other body/mind-altering influences that disrupt the body's harmony and connection to themselves and their Spirit. At points in my life, I disrespected this life vehicle of the body. In a synchronic way, my posture changed my attitude toward myself and others, so I love the abilities I possess.

Six months after the surgery, I played on the varsity tennis team again. I received first place in a sprint triathlon eight months later. Two years later, I was incorporating strength training into my routine. As the years went by, I appreciated my body in diverse ways and didn't take all it does for me for granted. All those months spent in bed in a back brace and taking ten minutes to walk up fifteen steps helped me reawaken to the gift of the body. I noticed how I slouched over my phone or computer and soon used a standing desk. I realized the culture of sitting, which was ingrained in me from school. In the health field, they say, "Sitting is the new smoking," as it can lead to various health issues. One of these includes "tech neck," which can lead to headaches, neck and shoulder pain, and tingling and numbness in the hands. The surgery awakened a body awareness that changed the trajectory of my life.

The scar that I carry with me is not a sign of weakness, but strength. Some say that scars are like tattoos with better stories. When someone asks me about it, I say I'm an iron woman and try to joke about it to help people realize that this surgery is part of my physical identity in this lifetime. It is something I am not attached to or which I ignore. I care for it, as it helped me strengthen my relationship with myself. So when I hear people say they can't do yoga because they are not flexible or it's too hard, I share this story, and more times than not, they give yoga a try and come back months later with their own level of transformation. The body follows what the mind believes.

Mirror Mirror

To put it bluntly, we live in a culture that has developed programming to convince us to hate ourselves. The programming becomes lodged so deeply, from the familiar voices of family members to commercials on TV, that we start to believe this lie. A culture that criticizes, demonizes, and neglects the true meaning of loving yourself by shoving products down our throats that do not connect us to the love within. When you look in the mirror, what are your first thoughts? Do you say things in your head that you'd never say to a friend? Or do you praise and cherish the things that are beautiful about you? You can choose the thoughts you want to believe, and it is a practice to change your mind to align with the love inherent in all of us.

You realize how much you have when you are in situations where you no longer have your previous abilities. Whether it is plantar fasciitis in the foot or a torn ACL, I believe injuries and ailments change perspectives on abilities and your relationship with your body. They are teachers. They are blessings. "Slow down!" they say. "You are doing too much." Sometimes this inner voice quietly whispers: "You are supported."

Your inner voice reminds you when you feel helpless. When you look at yourself in the mirror in these challenging times, remember to connect to the message within your eyes. Those brilliant eyes of yours are a direct connection to your soul. Notice that your body is an interconnected system that you have a choice to take care of. You can focus your mind on healing and love instead of pain and fear. In many ways, healing starts with the mind and the perception of your situation. At first, I was very resistant to scoliosis surgery. Months after the surgery, I felt a blanket of fear lift off of me when I came to peace with it. Physical health and digital health are often not paired together, but from a holistic perspective, it is all connected. When I was home for a few months of healing, I spent more time watching television, working on the computer for school, and talking with people on my phone. I felt isolated, and technology made me fall under the illusion that I was connected. Some of it was helpful, like speaking to my best friend about the intense breakup she was going through. Other times, it was harmful, like the habits of late-night TV watching and texting at three in the morning. I didn't have boundaries with my screens, and they seeped into my daily tasks.

After I could leave the house and be active again, my phone traveled with me more. I slowly switched my screen habits to more interaction with the world, which felt awkward and brought up anxiety at first, similar to the feeling of post-pandemic interactions. The screen was my mask. When the healing from my surgery was almost to an end, I was left with addictive inclinations toward screens. A true example of this is my going everywhere with my phone and feeling anxious when I left it at home or lost it for some time. However, the one thing that improved was my posture. There was no slouching on the computer or tech neck from looking at the phone. I was more aware of my posture and how it impacted my inner world.

Scoliosis surgery changed the way I approached life, especially exercise and movement. There was a point in college when I pushed myself above any limits. I'd scroll mindlessly through the fitness pages I followed on social media and became obsessed with my physical image. My three to four workouts a week became a fascination with improving my physical appearance. The culture I was raised in compelled me to believe I wasn't good enough. The fitness and wellness pages I followed confirmed that message. As a result, I went in a direction I never saw myself going, bodybuilding.

Tech Step 4: Embody Physical Wellness

We've all heard the phrase "the struggle is real." In regard to your health, for many, it's a struggle to attain a balance between health and all the other things that give us instant gratification. A friend of mine works at a bank where she sits in front of the computer eight hours a day. For her, the struggle is real to get up or try not to look at a screen because those are part of her job.

Complete one or more of the following suggestions for ways to move closer to digital and physical wellness. These approaches will, in turn, help open you to more presence and awareness.

Note: I have found that my own barriers to the following wellness techniques arise not because I don't think they are fantastic and valuable but because they go against a cultural norm. These techniques test people's comfort levels in a good way. So when you say to yourself, "This won't be possible," or "People will think I'm weird," test these beliefs by completing one of these techniques and see their effect on your energy, connections, and life.

- Stand or walk when possible. Why not make it a walking meeting if someone wants to meet with you? Or stand during particular activities, like talking on the phone or walking after eating a meal.

- In your daily life, take small measures to move. For example, park further away when you go to the store or to work or school. In our culture, we tend to rush everywhere. While you move, pay attention to each step and the thoughts coming and going.

- Find ways to go outside, whether it is eating lunch or going on a walk during your break. Do this without a screen and look at what is around you.

- Create an ergonomic work/play environment. This may take some time yet has a long-lasting effect. Some examples of this are adding better lighting, some plants or crystals, an organized desk, an ergonomic chair, or a standing station. Another example is sitting on a stability ball instead of a chair, which can help develop your core. A change like this can considerably impact our physical and emotional well-being.

- This one is more of a spiritual movement and a simple one that takes less than a minute. Each morning when you get up, before you check your phone, say the simple prayer, "Spirit, move me." Three words, one result: alignment.

- When you are at your computer, set a timer and intention before opening it. Write the intention so you are less tempted to check your phone or get distracted. Set a timer for the allotted time, and when the timer dings, move your body and refocus. Being firm in your purpose will help you target what you choose to do with your time and energy. You will complete the task faster than when doing the same job with many distractions. What is your intention when you turn on your computer next time?

When you integrate one or more of these efforts into your routine and lifestyle, you are not only helping yourself but also positively changing a culture that encourages sitting and robotically staring at a screen. You are also using your body's power to uplift yourself and create energy.

When you put forth effort into having a sense of Self that inspires others, you lead not by judgment but by example. When you love, accept, and heal your body, you will be able to spread this love, acceptance, and healing to each moment of your day simply by being yourself, one movement at a time.

Chapter Five

Bodybuilding

It was a hot summer afternoon, and I went to the gym because this super-fit couple was talking about nutrition. I was one of three people who came. My brain was soaking in all the information they were giving me. After the talk, I got to know them and their passions for bodybuilding. That evening, I went home to follow fitness professionals on social media who posted filtered photos of their nearly perfect physiques. I was not out of shape, yet I'd learned to judge my body more than love it because of society's messages. What social media did not show was their mental health status or how they really thought about food or their bodies.

My first National Physique Committee bodybuilding competition with a personal trainer was in 2015. I stuck to a prescribed nutrition plan, counted my macros, and woke up at 4:30 a.m. for the gym most days, sometimes going twice a day. I got a job at the gym and a supplement shop in town. I had tunnel vision toward the next fitness competition. A vision pumped through my blood to put on my $300 bikini, step on stage, get first place, and show all my Instagram followers I am a beast. In the first year or two, I imagined becoming a pro and being sponsored to enter these costly competitions with free top-of-the-line fitness swag.

I received second place in my first competition with seventeen other girls. After the show, I relied on the three judges to tell me how I could look better. "Fill up in your glutes and legs," they told me. I trained with those words echoing in my head. I posted my progress pics on Instagram with many hashtags. I mainly competed for myself. But there were parts of me that thrived on approval from online followers, competition judges, peers, and friends. My perception of health as a young adult was being ripped, receiving online validation, and grinding so hard that, at the end of the day, I was exhausted.

While training for over a year, I invested heavily in studies during my second and third years of school. I spent hours studying with my gallon water jug next to me in front of a screen. If I wasn't doing that, I worked out at the gym. Having two metal rods in my back helped with my posture, but I still felt trapped behind a desk. I held my phone for an extended period, scrolling through posts that filled me with judgment and hurt my thumb, wrist, and forearm. Moving my body made me feel free, and I became much more aware of how technology, driving, and sitting affected my health.

I shifted these technology habits to adapt to how my body was asking for change. For the first time, I listened to my body, not the scolding inner voice of past teachers saying sit, be quiet, and focus. I was that girl who got up in a lecture and stretched, knowing that I would be more productive if blood was flowing to my brain. I was that person who walked around campus without headphones or looking at her phone because I just wanted to enjoy the walk. In my junior year of college, I asked my parents for a stand-up desk for the holidays and chose to work standing up every place I was employed.

I entered my second competition and received second place again. With little awareness of how my life would transform over the next few months, I joined a national qualifier competition. I placed fourth in that competition, one spot away from national qualifying. Afterward, I trained with a different coach, and I wanted to show people I could do anything I set my mind to. And I did, at the risk of eventually getting myself into a state of depletion, losing friends, losing my period, and developing an eating disorder. Thank Goddess the body, mind, and Spirit are forgiving and can heal.

Spiritual Reconciliation

My bodybuilding career didn't last long. After three years of competing, that same person who held the nutrition talk saw me in the bathroom one day and said, "You don't look well, Melissa. Your hair is thinning, and your skin is pale. Are you okay?" Immediately, I broke into tears. I looked at myself in the mirror and didn't recognize the person staring back. The person in the mirror wasn't me. That day, I stopped working with the coach I was training with. Weeks passed, and I saw a therapist who diagnosed me with an undiagnosed eating disorder called "orthorexia," defined as an obsession with healthy eating. This time, I started on a path of finding my True Self, by deleting my social media account and dipping my toes into the world of yoga and meditation.

I walked away from competitions, acknowledging there is more to life than how I look and that the intense training it took to be a pro wasn't for me. It took me years to heal, mostly mentally. To enjoy food without thinking about how many macros were in it was an accomplishment in and of itself. As was looking into the mirror and seeing I am so much more than my body image or the image I created on social media. I was redefining who I was, which started from a deep place within myself and journaling about my journey.

I didn't have a relationship with a Spirit or God(dess) before I started fitness competitions, or even before I filled my days with hours of screen time. It didn't even occur to me that a force outside of me was there to help. Moreover, I never thought about that same force living within myself, clarifying my love and creativity.

Then I started having this thing called faith. You've heard of it before, I'm sure. That undeniable attitude of trusting in yourself and something higher than you and surrendering to the small clues of wisdom trickled through inspiration, play, and curiosity that led to something greater than you've ever imagined. Yeah, that thing. It was there in front of my eyes, and I listened to that intuitive voice and my body's cues to show me the way.

That is when my relationship with something I didn't believe in most of my life came into existence. Once it exists, it is challenging to unknow that intimate relationship with the Divine. A new chapter began. The conscious part of the adulting I'd been doing emerged from the waters.

Adulting Lessons

When you become an adult, life, or the Universe, will repeatedly hand you lessons until you learn them. Some of these lessons can be harsh, but they're nothing you can't handle. Have you experienced a life lesson that frequently occurred until you either learned it directly or learned it from someone else?

My bodybuilding days taught me about those words you see in many self-help books in today's world. I discovered the meaning of body awareness, body acceptance, and listening to what the body truly needs. For so long, I ignored my body's signals to stop, rest, go out in nature, and simply slow down. That is all too common with how stimulated we are by tech in today's world.

I started practicing yoga and listening to spiritual talks that helped me recover from my obsession with healthy eating and social media, which I believe were connected. There were many days when I'd sit down at a table to have a meal on my own and want so badly to pick up my phone. This habit I created made me shovel food into my mouth without even tasting it. I practiced mindful eating, where you pay attention to the senses while eating a meal. After a few weeks of not having the phone with me at a meal, I didn't think about picking it up, and I still don't have it around while enjoying a meal with my partner or friends.

The journey to this radical idea we have everything we need within ourselves has shifted my perspective and continues to change me today. It is a lifelong experiment because the magnificent body is constantly changing, and it is our responsibility to listen to what it needs at this moment.

For now, it is enough for me to exercise by doing what I love: teaching yoga and cycling, playing tennis, lifting weights with friends, and enjoying nature walks and bike rides. I incorporate this variety of things that makes me feel good, knowing I have everything I need to love myself as I am.

In the modern world, the identity we create online is an extension of ourselves. Some people try to hide behind this identity, while others develop it authentically. As humans and spiritual beings, we are constantly changing and evolving, and if we want to act consciously in the world, then we must define this online identity on our own terms, not on modern culture's terms.

When you developed your online identity, why did you do it? I did it because everyone else was, and it evolved to represent my business. Whether on LinkedIn or TikTok, it is challenging not to have an online presence. Is this online version different from the real you? Have you had experiences where you have to build this fundamental faith or trust in yourself enough to know who that is?

Algorithm's Dark Magic

If you know anything about the internet, you know the ad for the shoes you were just texting your friend about can pop up on your feed in minutes. In a quote from the popular documentary *The Social Dilemma*, Tristan Harris, former design ethicist at Google and president of the Center for Humane Technology, speaks some truth that can be felt: "If something is a tool, it genuinely is just sitting there, waiting patiently. If something is not a tool, it's demanding things from you. It's seducing you, manipulating you, and wanting things from you. We've moved away from a tools-based technology environment to an addiction and manipulation technology environment. Social media isn't a tool waiting to be used. It has its own goals and its own means of pursuing them by using your psychology against you" (Orlowski-Yang 2020).

The algorithms and metrics weaved into the artificial intelligence of social sites like Instagram and Facebook are created to capture your attention. According to a new study by Harvard University, self-disclosure on social networking sites lights up the same part of the brain that ignites when taking an addictive substance. The reward area in the brain and its chemical messenger pathways affect decisions and sensations (Hilliard 2022).

This may be alarming if you have not questioned the content or the normalcy of picking up our phones out of habit. Having self-compassion for rewiring our brains, which are more intelligent than our smartphones, is crucial to changing these behaviors technology has programmed in us by design.

Conscious Adulting is a continual practice of discovering who you are and purposefully sharing that with the world. This doesn't mean you have to share everything. It means you are aware of your soul's depth and how you're showing up in the world, both in reality and digitally. We will explore the real you and the online you to relate to those images of yourself.

Tech Step 5: Real Me Vs. Online Me

Since I was a teenager, there has been this gap between the real, authentic, and online versions of myself. I wanted people to only see my life's fun and exciting parts online. The friends, the fun parties, my handsome boyfriend. I created this person online. That wasn't my whole authentic Self. Frankly, as a teenager in high school, I didn't know who my whole authentic Self was.

Have you ever thought about the reasons you use your Snapchat or Instagram? Have you ever thought about your intention when you scroll or add new friends? People who enter the world of social media create an identity based on selfies and screenshots. This curation is not the reality of a person, though some may perceive it as such. If we spend a lot of time online, our self-worth begins to depend on how many likes, shares, and comments we receive on our photos. If we aren't careful, we can get sucked into the world of self-validation from this online world. This happened to me when I engaged in fitness competitions. Before changing their social media habits, this also happened to my friend Raf and many others. This can lead to depression.

When we carefully curate this online identity, our online version of ourselves becomes different from our real one. We start to question who we are and what we are putting online.

Eventually, we begin to be this different version of ourselves. This next Tech Step aligns with shifting your perspective about showing up in your real life versus your online identity. I had to move my viewpoint to use social media in a way that was helping me grow instead of making me feel small. It doesn't matter what online platform you use; this can apply to any of them.

The perspective shift occurs by realizing your online presence is not a way to earn validation. Instead, an online presence is a way for us to express a part of ourselves while accepting it isn't all of who we are. It is not about giving up your quirks and the things that make you yourself. Actually, it is quite the opposite. Our real happiness will not come from social media. We depend on the moments that weave our lives to provide lasting enjoyment.

Step 1: Write five things that bring you joy in your life: Schedule one to three activities listed above in the next week. Commit to long-term happiness and fulfillment.

Step 2: Reflect on your social media image right now. Write how you view the image you have created for yourself.

Step 3: Answer these questions.

How does this image you've created represent who you are? What are the ways it doesn't?

What areas in your life might you avoid confronting because of the image you've represented on social media? How can you align your True Self with your online Self?

In addition to who you are choosing to be, there is also how you choose to use social media. Are you stopping at a red light to check your accounts? Or are you setting a time of day when you take time to connect with people?

Step 4: How do you use social media? Where are you? What are you doing when you pick up your phone or computer? How do you feel when you go on social media and scroll?

What step can you take to be more intentional with your time on social media during your day?

Step 5: Next time you post something on social media or judge someone else's post, remember:

You are a spiritual being.

People are constantly changing, including you.

You choose the person you are online, and remember that the relationship with yourself is more important than any social media image.

With this being said, allow space for yourself to grow. I encourage you not to attach to this online identity because you are constantly changing. And it is okay to take a break. I promise you won't miss anything too important.

My relationship with social media changed when I stopped bodybuilding and shifted to focus more on yoga and meditation after spending time away from social media. In the same way, focus on building your life based on looking within and reflecting on what you love and what moves you. Give yourself, your True Self, a space to be explored. The goal is to use social media to support your positive life habits and practices. With awareness of your current usage, you can be more authentic in your real life and understand who you indeed are.

Chapter Six

California Hippie

You might think of marijuana-smoking, free-spirited travelers when you think of hippies. Or you may think of a yogi who is a vegan foodie with hundreds of crystals and gems around their bungalow. After my bodybuilding phase, I lived my best hippie life adventure in California. I was neither of the above stereotypes, but I was over the school system and wanted freedom from society.

While still in Florida, yoga and meditation helped me heal and feel connected to a deep part of me I'd never accessed before. I went to The Temple of the Universe to hear talks by Michael Singer, the bestselling author of *The Surrender Experiment* and *The Untethered Soul*. Some of my family thought I was nuts, while other friends came with me to the Temple. I'd go into the large open cabin in the woods and bow down on the carpeted floor to their altar, filled with spiritual beings, flowers, and the energy of love and devotion. Patiently, I'd take a seat on the cushion and wait for the music to start and for Michael (Micky) to give his talk on topics like letting go and basic spiritual principles.

I did this for months as I waited for an internship to start in California. This internship was with one of the most successful workplace wellness directors in America, Mitch Martens, at Cedars-Sinai Hospital. I was to complete my degree at the University of Florida in health education and behavior with this internship. Plus, Mitch was someone I looked up to, and I admired his outlook and enthusiasm for his work.

One week before I planned to leave for California, I got a call from the director of the health education department while I was at a friend's house. "Melissa, I am sorry to inform you, but we made a mistake in your credit hours, and you actually need three more credits to do your internship.

We have some online courses you can take that I can help you get enrolled in them. Please call me when you can."

For a few hours, I was devastated. It took everything in me to practice resilience and bounce back to take another course of action. Over the next few days, I arranged to stay with my family in Santa Cruz, California, until the internship started four months later. I signed up for an introductory nutrition class to get the three credits I needed. I trusted in a bigger plan and that the pathway was proceeding to where I needed to be to grow.

I drove to California with a friend who I didn't know well. By the third day, I was ready to stop smelling his stinky armpits and hearing his music that sounded like screaming monkeys—test number one from the Universe on this journey. After the cross-country expedition, I arrived at my family's house, and I thanked them for allowing me to stay there. I unloaded my stuff into a room already filled with dolls, books, and objects that didn't belong to me. Although it didn't feel like home, it still felt nice to receive support from family.

Days into my stay, I started my course and looked for a part-time job. At that same time, I found a yoga studio a walk away from my relative's home, in this cute shopping center next to a bakery. One day, the teacher mentioned something about yoga teacher training, and I felt in my body an undeniable *yes*. It was a three-week intensive, costing almost the exact amount I had saved.

I spent the money and enrolled in the course the next day. It was one of the best investments I ever made in myself. For three weeks, fifteen of us from around the world met in a space a block away from the Santa Cruz ocean. On the third week of the training, I packed up my things and moved to an eco-village.

The internship was the last thing on my mind. In fact, all I desired was to teach yoga and live off the grid in this eco-village. I stayed a few weeks and completed my yoga training and watched the marijuana cultivation and packaging process occur before my eyes. Travelers passed through and cooked food for the other people coming and going, exchanging conversations about music, health, and life. After meeting some of the most magical people, with names like Artimus, I left the mountains and listened to my intuition telling me to go to Berkeley, California, to figure out my next steps.

This type of travel was not familiar to me. I grew up with trips over-planned, rushing to the next thing and the next. The spontaneity and uncertainty of this trip gave me the freedom to deeply trust myself. This type of travel was not a way to get lost but a way to find myself.

The Box

I found a place to stay with four roommates and six dogs, where I slept on a cot in a large laundry room and paid $450 for rent. I brought in the first box from my car, which said, "Follow your dreams. They know the way." Following my twenty-two-year-old hippie dreams felt freakin' scary. I've never been so far away from my home in Florida on my own. I felt anxious about living with so many people in a foreign place, with a big question mark for my future.

Before I unpacked my stuff, stashed strategically in the back of my Honda Hatchback, I sat down in my new bedroom with this dream box and opened it. The smell of sage brushed my nostrils. Inside this box were sacred objects I collected on my life journey. I had sticks, feathers, crystals, photos of people that uplifted me, a few candles, sage, a small statue of Ganesha—the Hindu elephant god—and other treasures.

Carefully, I picked each item up, set them on the floor, closed the box, and strategically placed each of them on top of the box as I connected to the meaning of each object.

I lit the sage and swayed it around my newly formed altar, passing by the cot, the washer and dryer, and the door to the backyard. I bowed my head in front of the altar and took deep breaths. The little child inside me who felt scared grew more courageous. Still, tears fell from my eyes, and my memory flashed back to the yoga training, eco-village, and events that aligned me to being right there.

I trusted this was exactly where I needed to be. My state of emotions altered as I released my worries and let in trust in the unknown. Love and protection surrounded the space.

I set up that altar countless times, once even for a weekend vacation at a hotel. It represented a coming home to something higher than me. By taking charge of my own well-being and internal stability, I would give that back to others and the planet. I often walked into the door of the overstimulated house, past the living room TV noise, through the tiny kitchen, and straight to my bedroom and threw myself down on the ground at the altar, processing my day and returning to love. At times, I'd stay for ten minutes, sometimes crying from loneliness or laughing with joy. This altar box was my way to release and return to my most profound truth, my understanding of God or the Universe.

An Alternative

Growing up, the practice was reaching for my phone when I really craved a deeper connection with myself and the Universe. I'd pick it up to check the latest addictive app, seeing if connection was hiding in the algorithms. Though when I looked up, I felt lonelier than before. My device was there to easily text someone who would give me love and affection years ago, like an old boyfriend or friend. Empty conversations didn't last long because they held only stale emotions from the past.

As a child, the alternative to hearing Spirit was hearing noises of the altar set up in the middle of our living room, the television. It was the centerpiece in many Americans' homes, the first thing we'd bow down to after a long day of school or work. Even though there were times we spent kayaking and playing outside, a TV was in every bedroom, and technology was integrated into the lifestyle our family lived. As I got older, I knew there had to be a balance. I heard the same stories from people who said, "I'm not getting enough sleep," or "I am addicted to my phone!" I knew there was an alternative, a way of life that valued in-person connections and boundaries within the household. It was right in front of me.

Digital Feng Shui

The screens easily distracted me from that godly connection and faith. When I learned about altars at The Temple of the Universe, it was around the time I started practicing digital feng shui, though without realizing it. As defined by the Digital Wellness Institute (n.d.), "Digital feng shui brings balance to digital spaces by using principles from ancient Chinese practices that build upon nature's flow and ability to neutralize energy and enhance positive energy."

When I left fitness competitions, I adopted a minimalist lifestyle, which included reducing tech use. For about a year, I used a flip phone instead of an iPhone. I dropped the online identity I created through social media and spent my evenings in solitude or with friends instead of on Netflix. I spent car rides in silence and many hours in nature. It was an extreme shift, but it helped me redefine and listen to this person I had never clearly known and this connection to the values I chose to live in my life. There wasn't this feeling of digital overwhelm, where things constantly came at me that stole my attention. At that point, I added key elements to enhance my values and removed things not serving the person I was becoming. Like clearing a space, I also added in a digital-clutter clean. My desktop contained icons, emails I'd stored for years, and documents of little importance. Each clearing helped me make space for things that mattered, like friendships and traveling.

I added a charging station, where our devices live most of the time when we are in my house. And, as you may suspect, the altar came into my life and held as the centerpiece for coming home to myself and to Spirit. Now, my grandfather's piano is in our living room, a reminder of creativity in our home.

What creates the most value in your life? Is it writing? Is it your children? Is it nature? How does your home reflect your inner world, and what brings you fulfillment and joy?

Although I made some drastic changes, it is not something I recommend in a short amount of time unless you feel 100 percent ready for that. But perhaps you feel inspired to make a change toward digital wellness in your home. How might one go about all these changes?

There is an abundance of self-compassion and patience involved, especially if you were like me, who slept with my phone by my side and had the TV as an altar. However, change is possible when you trust you know what is best for you and take it one step at a time.

Tech Step 6: Altar of Love

You may already have a religious or spiritual practice that connects you to a higher source, God, or any other spirit or guide you honor. You may not believe in a "god" or higher power. Whatever your viewpoint, the experience of meditation can be undeniably helpful to anyone.

If you feel this digital overwhelm, how can you spend time getting to know this inner process if you are too busy? Distractions will appear while diving into a self-care technique. It is a blessing that a self-care practice is practically built into you as a human, a mammal, a living being—it is innate. Your power is being in charge of your own well-being. You hold the key to your own process. Therefore, an environment that makes it easy to develop a relationship with this inner technology is essential. There are two types of external spaces that can clear the way for personal growth:

1. Physical Spaces

2. Digital Spaces

Physical Spaces: Creating an Altar

Out of all the places to start decluttering, my personal suggestion is to begin with an altar.

The altar is a way of sending a text message to the Universe, or God. God would text back, saying something simple and to the point. *Honey Bee, you are precisely where you need to be.*

This connection maintained my openness so I could detach from my initial plan to go to Cali for the internship. The Universe was guiding me in another direction, one that was better than I could have ever imagined.

What you will need:

- Journal and pen
- Small table or stand (if traveling, place things in a small box)
- Candle(s) or incense
- Pictures of spiritual beings that you admire (Jesus, Buddha, Gurus, teachers in your past)
- Flowers or plants (optional)
- Objects that are sacred to you (i.e., stones, crystals, singing bowl, quotes)
- Meditation cushion or pillow, yoga mat, sheepskin mat, or blanket
- Quiet time during the morning or evening

Step 1. Do you see that pile of useless stuff in the corner which you never use or use once a year? Get rid of it! This is your meditation space. When we declutter our external space, our internal space automatically clears.

Step 2. Practice non-judgment. Assure yourself this is going to help you self-initiate a better life. "I completely love and accept myself. I am doing this for myself."

Step 3. Buy any supplies with joy because you are improving yourself #selfcare. (Going to a thrift shop or reusable material store is encouraged.)

Step 4. Set up an altar, a sacred sanctuary in a space that enables you to ground, connect, and grow. The altar helps alter consciousness.

Step 5. Block out time when you will be able to sit for ten to twenty minutes with no distractions. The more consistent you are the better. However, start slow. If three times a week is realistic to begin, start there. Be gentle with yourself.

Step 6. Be transparent with the people you live with by saying, "This is my meditation time, and please respect it by not disturbing me." Turn your phone on silent and only use it for a timer or for music to help facilitate your practice.

Step 7. Give yourself permission to follow the journaling questions and meditations presented in this book. Some may take you days to contemplate and experience. Be patient with yourself.

Voilà! You have a spiritual space (or small spiritual box) to connect with meditation, yoga, creativity, or prayer.

Digital Spaces:

Digital spaces are more complicated because we all use them differently. Perhaps we have twenty apps on our phone, with only six we use regularly. Or maybe you have 262 unopened emails in your inbox, and you feel overwhelmed every time you check your email. Perhaps you are checking your email too often and creating an unhealthy cycle so you can respond in record time. A yoga teacher I know mentioned the digital space she needs to clear are her thousands of photos, mostly of her dog.

Ask yourself the questions below, responding honestly. Then decide on how you will take action to clear your digital space.

Have you ever looked at _____? Do you really need _____? Is _____ promoting my well-being?

Here Are Some Digital Declutter Tips:

Weekly Digital Laundry: Set aside a time each week when you partake in the digital laundry, decluttering emails, texts, and other items crowding your digital space.

Seasonal Clearing: At the beginning of each season, look through your communication channels and declutter anything not relevant to your current Self.

Email: Clear your email. Take one hour to start from the beginning of your email, clear anything unnecessary, and place the essential things in folders. To start, pick a subsection in your email and work from there.

Social Media: Look at the images you have and your profile photo. Take out the things that no longer reflect who you are in the present.

Televisions: Turn off autoplay so you are not constantly watching things that are not planned. Watch in the presence of others and with intention.

Reminder: Enjoy the victories and celebrate living with more purpose and fewer things impeding your seeing and enjoying the True You. Connecting even once a week with your newly formed altar can give you the energy you need to propel into the world with a more profound connection with your inner and outer technology.

Chapter Seven

Why I Hug a Tree

I share this next story about coming into a world where "What is normal?" is questioned almost daily. We build ourselves based on the idea that we must act a certain way and mold ourselves into what society views as "normal." To some extent, we choose to comply with rules and regulations for our safety and well-being. At other times, we imagine stories about what others think and make decisions about our own lives based on that. I judged myself for my connection to nature until, one day, I embraced it. Has there been a moment when you've accepted an aspect of yourself that you judged in the past and which makes you feel whole and complete today? Whether it is a sexual orientation or a career change to something you love. Is there a moment of decision that helped you remember who you truly are?

Tree Hugger

I rushed out the door one morning with my purple rolling backpack I bought a few weeks before in Chinatown. The kind of backpack that was cool in fourth grade was now handy for living in the city. It was a windy day in Oakland, California, where I moved after my California-hippie phase. The breeze switched back and forth from biting to forgiving and back to biting like a playful dog. I walked down a steep Oakland street faster than my body wanted to, then down a dirt cut-through path, took a left, and power walked to the bus stop, just in time for the bus to pull up. When I got on the bus, I sat next to a plump Asian lady who looked like she got as little sleep as I had last night. I smiled at her, and she looked at me as if she was saying, "I'm not here to make friends, just trying to support my family." I took a breath and turned away.

This was the fourth week of my internship at a new Wellness Center in Downtown Oakland. I chose this option instead of the hospital where I originally planned to intern because I perceived this company as being more aligned with my career path at the time. As I sat tensely on the bus, I pulled out my phone for the first time all morning and saw a text message from my boss: "I'll be at work by 9 to open the doors. Our first client is at 10 today. See you then."

Usually, I start work at 8:30 a.m. It was 8:00 a.m. I sat there, holding my backpack close, feeling my jaw tighten and my fist clench my phone a little tighter. I remembered what I did last time this happened. Instead of sitting at the front door tired and resentful, this time I would go on an adventure around my workplace.

I relaxed and rode the rest of the bus ride, smelling the intense fragrance of perfumes and gazing out the blurry bus window, imagining where I would go. I got off the bus and walked to the office, reassuring myself no one was there. The door was locked, and the lights were off. If I had entered then, my morning would have started on an iPad or computer, with me holding it together around the buzz of Downtown Oakland. The internship was more structured than my wild and free twenty-one-year-old Spirit envisioned when coming out to California. There is nothing like those deceiving Instagram pictures of fit twenty-somethings doing yoga on the beach. If I had been honest with myself from the beginning of this internship/job, I would have seen the signs of a controlling boss and acknowledged the weird vibes.

I was determined to finish school and release the pressure of society, my parents, and my own ideas of what success meant. Some days, the anxiety would manifest as disregarding my health and spending hours on a screen, numbing myself, or ignoring inner and outer pain. Anxiety would also display itself through disconnection from my friends and feelings.

The pressure made my soft, calm face stiffen into who the world wanted me to be. My eyes would widen, my body hunch forward, my breath and attention span shorten, and I'd shrink. I knew that version of me was not the depth of who I indeed was. My expansive nature felt the limited parameters of a rectangular piece of technology. I shrank small enough to fit the molds, ideas, fads, and opinions of what was happening on that device and in the blur of life around me.

When I was at work, I'd occasionally feel connected to the bright screen and what I was doing, forgetting. I'd forget I am in this human body, and I have needs. I failed to drink water, go to the bathroom, or listen to my body's signals. The screen did a great job of marketing and convincing me that my needs were being met. At the core, though, I needed breaks to get quiet and ask myself what would fill me up. "Am I the only one who feels this way?" I'd ask myself.

Arriving at the office an hour earlier that day, I took it as a sign that I needed space. I stood at the office door and looked down at my phone, seeking distraction and a sense of control. I opened Facebook without much thought. Then, I realized this impulsive move, put my phone away in my bag, and started walking toward Grand Lake a few blocks away. I stopped at the light and waited to cross. I smiled at the guy next to me, who had headphones and his phone in his hand. He smiled back. We were forced into a moment of stillness as we waited for the light. He looked at his phone. I kept an eye on the crosswalk. When the light turned, I continued at a moderate, city-like pace. I made eye contact and flashed a fabricated smile at people going by. Most of them had headphones in or looked up and down from a cell phone while walking at a breakneck pace, much faster than my wannabe city gal stride. Rushing to wait. Hurrying to sit. I felt and lived those feelings most mornings.

Then, I stepped foot on the path that circles Grand Lake. I walked for a few minutes before veering off the sidewalk into the grass close to the water. First, I stepped in with shoes. Then, a moment later, with shoes in my hands and bare feet on the cool grass glazed with morning dew. At that moment, my need for connection and security was met. I needed to be still. I needed more than to be still. I needed to feel. I needed to feel the ground beneath me and the internal feeling that everything was okay.

Joggers, walkers, and people with briefcases sped by while I felt the grass tingle my feet. The serene breeze lifted off the water and into my hair. Then, without much thought, I walked over to the tree next to me, the most stable thing I knew at that moment, wrapped my arms around it, placed my forehead against its rough bark, and took about five deep breaths. With each breath I took, I felt that buzzing feeling dissipate. On the inhale, the voice of judgment tried to sneak in. When exhaling, I let that voice go, seeping into the tree's bark and sinking into the ground below a little more. The voice of anxiety and anger from my morning turned into a song of calmness. I heard nothing but nature and cars in the distance. I felt my shoulders soften, my breaths deepen, my jaw relax, and my mind return to those expansive, loving thoughts that felt like home. I remembered I was alive.

I felt connected to myself once again and connected to nature. I remembered. I remembered my own needs. I remembered my connection to nature brings me back to my center, a place of knowing and calmness. It connected me to something higher than me. After stepping away and putting my shoes back on, I laughed aloud at what I had just done. I hugged a tree with my bare feet on the earth while most of the people surrounding me were in the buzz of their morning: buzzed on coffee, cell phone stimulation, and anxiety. And I just hugged a tree. "Wow, I'm a damn hippie! And I am myself," I thought to myself, in acceptance.

It didn't matter what my label was, though. "Hippie," "tree-hugger," "yogi," etcetera. I felt energized, and the fake smile I gave to people on my way to Grand Lake turned into a genuine smile of ease. I got to the office a few minutes before my boss showed up with a warm drink in one hand and his cell and keys in the other.

"Good morning! You're glowing!" he said to me as he opened the door to the office.

I smiled authentically. In my heart, I knew that my glow was from the gift of spending time in nature. Part of me wanted to say back to him, "You're buzzing!"

Power of Nature

How do you connect with yourself again after a device fails to connect you? How do you plug into yourself and recharge your own battery? That morning, when I hugged a tree, I surrendered to the playful possibilities that I would have never found scrolling through my phone. It brought me back to an inner screen that showed me physical, mental, emotional, and energetic balance. Nature helped me spray that internal screen clear of the anxiety, panic, and overwhelm I experienced almost daily after a few hours of being in front of my devices.

I used nature as a way to heal. The day my grandmother passed away, I drove to a state park and hiked for an hour. When I graduated from school, I went on a road trip and stayed in the mountains of North Carolina. I found peace in the soothing waters of natural springs and ocean waves. Even on a lunch break, I'd sneak away and walk barefoot down a small trail near the office. Nature brought me to a different type of "online"—one that recharged my inner battery and switched-on creativity and meaningful connection.

Almost like a radio frequency being tuned to the correct station, I tuned in to a path of purpose and direction when I felt lost. It helped me release the tech tension built up in my shoulders and neck. Various studies indicate nature helps with sleep habits, increases happiness, and reduces stress and negative emotions. Being in green environments boosts multiple aspects of thinking—including attention, memory, and creativity—in people with and without depression (Franco, Shanahan, and Fuller 2017).

There is a power in nature that isn't seen but felt. In a culture where we consume a Digital Diet of information, spending time in green spaces helps you clear and create.

With an inner compass pointing at clarity, one can hear what is calling them back to their soul.

Tech Step 7: Grounded and Stable

This Tech Step is about staying grounded. "Grounded" is a word that gets thrown around when verbalizing spiritual or yogic topics. Grounded refers to an internal and external feeling. It means you are in a stable emotional, mental, and spiritual state. "Externally grounded" means a feeling of internal balance and security resulting from an action. To be grounded means you are satisfied, centered, and in the present moment.

Groundedness relates to mindfulness, which spiritual junkies use when paying attention to the present moment. In *Shadow, Self, Spirit*, author Michael Daniels (2021) states groundedness refers to "a sense of being fully embodied, whole, centered and balanced in ourselves and our relationships." It's also a deeper connection to the authentic Self (Daniels 2021). He explains groundedness is associated "with an experience of clarity, wholeness, 'rightness' and harmony" (Daniels 2021).

This step does not involve technology. So we can call this a tech(no) step. Though there are no raging techno beats, it will provide ease when managing your outer technology while getting grounded.

Duration: 5–10 minutes

Step 1: Writing

Write about a time when you've felt uneasy or ungrounded. What did that feel like in your body? What were your thoughts? Are you still sitting with that feeling? How did you handle it? Was there something that put you at balance?

Step 2: Actionable

In that situation where you usually feel your depression, anxiety, anger, or your emotional fire spike, the desire comes up to act out of these emotions. In this unstable situation, what is the way you ground yourself? Try one of the following:

Calming Breath: Breathe in slowly and evenly, hold the breath as long as possible, then breathe out slowly and control. You can choose to breathe out of your mouth or nose.

Hug a Tree: Go outside with shoes on or barefoot and place your feet on an earthly surface. Find a tree nearby and wrap your arms around it. Stand there for at least a minute. Feel the earth beneath you and be present with your senses. Release anything you are holding on to. Feel held by nature's calming presence.

Affirmation: *I am grounded. I am alert. I am energized. I am mindful.*

Repeat this affirmation ten times out loud to yourself in a mirror.

Embodiment Exercises: Movement that awakens your awareness of the internal sensations and responses of the body is an excellent way to connect more to your inner home. During a recent yoga class I taught, I used the practice of connecting how the body feels when you answer an obvious Yes question and No question. Then, after noting what it feels like in the body when you answer these questions, ask a question you are unsure about and feel how the body's wisdom responds. There are various embodiment activities you can access on the resources page at the back of this book or on my website: MelissaHoneyBee.com

Step 3: Reflection

Noticing what makes you feel ungrounded is the first step to change. Commit to a way to ground yourself that aligns with your values. It was an hour of the morning spiritual alignment, along with feeling the bark of a tall tree. My weekly ritual is going on at least one nature walk. What is it for you?

Daily, I will feel grounded and centered by _____.

Weekly, I will feel grounded and centered by _____.

Chapter Eight

Returning to
Nature's Cycles

W e are all on a unique healing journey, and conscious adulting illuminates places lodged in our bodies and minds, and even our ancestral roots call for our healing. This journey is lifetimes long, though there may be times in life when you go deeper into the spiritual work. Often, we have to choose to listen to those signs telling us to slow down, rest, and look inward. When we do this, we can tune into the cycles of life. The cycles of the seasons, the moon, and even the cycles of each day are precious, and we can use them to enhance the quality of our health and relationship to our Spirit.

There was a clear sign for me to pay attention to nature's cycles in my early twenties. When my friends in my college program started talking about what they were going to do after they were done with school, I hesitated to answer. Each of them had a plan, from moving to go to grad school to working for the health department. I steered far away from the mainstream job selection in my field. I knew what I didn't want. I didn't want to feel trapped at a desk like my friend Angela did for twelve years. I didn't want to work with sick or end-of-life patients, even though I cared for my ninety-two-year-old grandmother a year after graduating. I knew I didn't want to spend my days working tirelessly until my inner fire burnt out.

Two weeks after I graduated from school, I went to Israel on a yoga and mindfulness birthright trip. A birthright trip is a practically free opportunity to visit Israel if you were born Jewish. With no commitments back in the United States, I decided to extend my ten-day trip and stay for two months. The culture, the food, the people, the places, the scenery, all of it was a divinely crafted dream. I stayed in various locations along the way, from the homes of people I met spontaneously to an ashram in the desert.

At the ashram, I did a work-trade program, where I attended the twice-daily meditations and yoga and worked during the day in the kitchen or doing laundry. Besides the radiant people, the most significant part of my experience in the ashram was healing my body.

A few years before I went to Israel, I trained for fitness competitions. At the same time, there was no monthly ovulation. No moon cycle, period, bleeding, whatever you like to call that monthly womanly cycle. Having no moon cycle is typical among female athletes. When I stopped doing the competitions two years later, my cycle did not return, and I was left feeling broken when a month came and went without a natural rhythm.

One full moon evening, I stood in the desert after the daily meditation, crying tears that felt moist dripping down my face against the dry air and wind blowing sand under my toes. Around the full moon is when I feel especially emotionally sensitive. I was crying out for healing, for answers to the vital questions, "Who am I" and "Why am I here?" I cried for all the people who lived before me, my ancestors whose pain and suffering were energetically passed down. It felt so good to wail out to the open desert, mainly because I was raised associating crying with weakness or ugliness. I was shedding layers buried deep within my bones, and it felt liberating, mending, and even empowering.

The following day, I woke up and went to the bathroom. I sat on the toilet and looked at the ray of dust from a shadow of light cracked through a window in the communal living space where I was staying. I wiped and glanced down at the toilet paper only to see a light red spot on the toilet paper. I'd received my cycle. I went to the communal kitchen to get some tea, and a person traveling from Australia also came into the kitchen.

"Good morning," I spoke softly, holding in my excitement, an excitement that I had never felt before about receiving my period. I couldn't hold it in any longer, and I had to tell someone. "Can I share something with you?" I asked with a childlike glow in my eye.

"Sure." She did a half-smile and looked me in the eye, available to hear what I was going to say.

"Today is the first day I have received my moon cycle in three years." My eyes started watering, and I wasn't holding back the tears this time.

"Oh, Honey!" she exclaimed and opened up her arms to hold me. "That is so special. I'm so happy for you!" Even if she didn't want to hear the story, I still told her, feeling like I was still processing what it took for me to get to this day. The days after, I gave myself plenty of time to rest, connect with women, and take care of myself as if this time was sacred.

Israel is where my spiritual path grew in depth. I was able to go deeper within myself and look through the eyes of wonder, faith, and healing. From that day on, I no longer viewed my cycle as some evil, gross, and annoying thing that happened in my body. It is a treasure that helps me slow down, connect with my intuition, and trust in the cycles of nature.

After three weeks in the desert, I extended my trip ten days and boldly signed up for a Kundalini yoga training in a small village outside Tel Aviv. Over the week of the training, I fell in love with the science of yoga all over again. I began to trust in the body's cycles again, which gave me a deeper faith in my body to heal and in nature to help me with the process.

Honoring the Cycles

Ayurveda, the sister science of yoga, arrived in the western world in the 1970s and '80s from India. In Sanskrit, "Ayurveda" breaks down to "Ayu," which means life or live life, and "Veda," which means knowledge. It is the knowledge of life. As in my yoga practice, I have taken principles from Ayurveda and applied them to my own life. There are various angles and concepts that Ayurveda teaches, some of which I still am trying to understand. I do not consider myself an Ayurveda expert, but I sincerely believe in the ancient wisdom passed down from guru to guru.

The part that touches my core and helps me connect to my own cycles relates to the Ayurvedic approach to nature. We may be aware of how nature's cycle influences our lives, from the seasons to the food that grows in the ground beneath us. According to this ancient science, our body's well-being correlates to the harmony between the elements (earth, air, fire, water, ether) in our bodies and minds. These elements make up our constitution. Our constitution consists of a balance of the three doshas: Vata, Pitta, and Kapha.

Vata consists of the elements of air and ether.

Pitta consists of the elements of fire and water.

Kapha consists of the elements of water and earth.

Here is a chart that explains the qualities of the doshas:

Dosha Qualities

Vata   Dry, Light, Cold, Rough, Subtle, Mobile, Clear

Pitta   Hot, Sharp, Light, Liquid, Spreading, Oily

Kapha   Heavy, Slow, Cool, Oily, Smooth, Dense, Soft, Stable, Gross, Cloudy (Sticky)

These three doshas can be seen in all existence, even in different organs of our body. Understanding what your dosha was when you were born, known as your "Prakruti," and where you are currently out of balance ("Vikruti") can be a helpful detriment of how to bring you back into balance.

Like the Ayurveda Health Retreat in Alachua, Florida, Ayurvedic centers worldwide help individuals heal from physical, mental, emotional, and energetic imbalances. You may be curious to know what dosha you are. If so, you can visit an Ayurvedic practitioner for the best results or take a dosha quiz online from chopra.com/dosha-quiz.

I have spent years teaching, volunteering, and participating in the Ayurveda Health Retreat's services and have seen transformative results in myself and my guests. In the resources section at the end of this book, you will find various books and trusted sources to dive more into the science of Ayurveda. If Ayurveda isn't something that resonates with you, there may be another mode of healing calling to your soul. Now is the time to listen, because when your body is in harmony with your soul, and your soul is in harmony with nature, you expand. As I mentioned at the beginning of this chapter, healing is a lifelong journey, and when you're able to emerge from the depths of dis-ease, you can create more ease and harmony within your life. What cycles can you connect with to awaken a deeper connection to yourself and life?

Tech Step 8: Healing & Nature's Cycles

Nature is always giving you signs. It is up to you whether to pay attention or walk right past them. I suggest this next Tech Step to bring you back into balance, whether you are walking or sprinting through life. Below is a list of four different ways to tune into nature's cycles, using the principles of Ayurveda and other ancient practices. If you are already doing them, fantastic! If these seem out of your routine, open up to new ways of interacting with life. Either way, I invite you to slow down, connect to an aspect of nature you have not yet harmonized with, and create a relationship with it. Create a sacred practice around it. Listen to the wisdom of our bodies and this Universe.

1. Stimulate the senses with nature and awe

We mainly use two senses when using a screen: sight and touch. When we are in nature, we can stimulate all our senses, which can help support our nervous system (Eating for the Ecosystem Applied Research and Education 2020). A robust study done in 2019 found spending two hours in nature improved health and well-being (White et al. 2019).

Spend time in green spaces without your device, and nurture all of your senses. There may be a message in the wind or the drops of rain softly dropping on your skin. Not only go on a walk outside with your dog but also look around and be childishly curious. Be more than mindful; expand into the wonder of nature.

2. Stop fighting your body, and ecstatically dance!

Because we live in an intense masculine world, sometimes we try to push ourselves to move more than our bodies want. Our society teaches us to be everything else except who we are. But what if you started paying attention to your emotions and your body's signals and honoring all these parts of you? You can do this by dancing, traveling, journaling, or walking in nature. Your body is starving for your love and acceptance. What can you do today to listen?

What if you were to put on your dancing pants and, with no substances, soberly move around your home as if no one was watching? Some cities host "ecstatic dances." These are conscious gatherings where people choose to move or not move in the way their bodies crave. This type of dancing helps us shed self-judgment, connect with other people, and move soulfully.

3. Ayurveda and the times of day

Have you noticed that you feel sluggish around 6:00 p.m.? Well, in Ayurveda, that is the Kapha part of the day. Ayurveda breaks the days into Pitta, Vata, and Kapha parts of the day.

Vata: 2–6 a.m./p.m.

Kapha: 6–10 a.m./p.m.

Pitta: 10–2 a.m./p.m.

If you want to align with the times of the day, you can do some of the following things to ensure you are making the most of this cycle.

To align yourself with the daytime Kapha cycle:

- Be up at or before sunrise. Sleeping in can increase tiredness or stiffness.

- Engage in some movement in the morning hours. It could be physical labor, yoga, or a cardiovascular workout.

- Eat breakfast, but be careful not to overeat at this meal, because that can likely increase Kapha.

To align yourself with the daytime pitta cycle:

- Make lunch the biggest meal of the day, but do not eat in front of a screen.

- Try your best to make most of the meal with seasonal foods.

- Rest for 10–15 minutes after the meal.

To align yourself with the daytime Vata cycle:

- Evaluate how you feel in the afternoon.

- Try to make lunch a more satisfying and balanced meal if you have cravings during this time.

- Meditate during the last part of this cycle between 5:00 p.m. and 6:00 p.m. If this is not realistic for your schedule, carve out time for a warm shower or a one-minute reset.

4. Moon Bathing

Our ancestors saw that the lunar cycle governs the menstrual cycle. Interestingly, the twenty-nine-day lunar cycle closely resembles the length of the menstrual cycle. Since the moon was our ancestors' only nighttime light source, what if you went outside in the evening more? Moon bathing during the full moon is one of my favorite ways to honor the moon cycle. A power happens when the moon's light touches your skin. If this isn't accessible to you, try creating some ritual around the moon or your menstrual cycle.

Chapter Nine

Digital Wellness

I was fifteen when I had my first serious boyfriend, Kevin. He was two years older than me and drove me around in his Ford truck. For about a year and a half, I felt like I was in a country love song. We'd go out on his boat early Saturday mornings, and I'd use the pink fishing rod that lit up when I reeled it in, which he gifted me one Christmas. We said "I love you" to each other, because after two months, this is what boyfriends and girlfriends do, right? There would be nights when we would text all night and times when I told my parents I was going over to a friend's house, and I'd go over to his house to watch a movie, snuggle, and get in stupid fights that would send me home crying. I'd call my friend for comfort, and she'd repeatedly listen to the same story.

Eventually, Kevin and I broke up, then got back together, and broke up again to shift to a cordial friendship. Soon after our relationship ended, I was scrolling online and found a picture of him and another girl. Jealousy and comparison kicked in, and I stalked her on social media and thought of why I was better than her. Then, I'd talk about it with my friends, calling this innocent girl names she did not deserve. Maliciously, I'd take photos with a guy friend of mine, feeling the jealousy loop until I'd felt like I'd "won." That was not the right way to handle it, but is anything the "right way" when you're a teenager?

I find that same jealous feeling creeping in years later, not toward Kevin or the person he is dating. I feel it, though, when I go on social media and see my friend living like a hippy minimalist in her pimped-out travel trailer or my other entrepreneur friend next to her Tesla. The story I was telling myself was "I'm not good enough," and it sucked me in, taking away my energy without my permission. I notice my mental and emotional health become compromised, and I exhaust myself until all I can do is believe that false story of "I am not doing enough or being enough in the world."

"Hey! Come back here with my attention and energy!" I wanted to say to my phone, but it ran away, and that hour of my life was gone. I felt emptier instead of more whole. Over time, I've learned to catch this toxic habit at the beginning of its life cycle. I have learned to understand the triggers that urge me to go to my phone as if I depend on it for my emotional security. I did not practice digital wellness as a teenager, and I learned what it meant to me when I became aware that I go to my email and social media when I feel lonely or want to avoid a challenging task. "Digital wellness" is a term I added to a wellness model that identifies six areas of health. This model includes physical, mental, emotional, spiritual, social, and environmental health.

When I learned these six areas of health in school, I was also looking around at the class of forty students. More than half were on their phones or an irrelevant website as the teacher talked. Something was missing, and this something was our digital health. Digital wellness affects each of these areas of our health. I've already mentioned some of these areas in previous chapters, like our physical health and mental health. Others, like our environmental health, may not be as obvious.

My phone buzzes next to me at my charging station as I'm writing, and I want so badly to look at it. This automatic response happens even when I'm driving. We can give our attention to our phones, computers, or Netflix or utilize our time as though it is sacred.

Nir Eyal and Julie Li-Eyal (2020) mention in the book *Indistractable*, "We can cope with uncomfortable internal triggers by reflecting on, rather than reacting to, our discomfort. We can reimagine the task we're trying to accomplish by looking for the fun in it and focusing on it more intensely. Finally, and most importantly, we can change the way we see ourselves to get rid of self-limiting beliefs."

The relationship we create with technology and the energy we give to it shape our digital well-being. Even though I am not perfect, there are moments when I give too much of myself away to these devices and give into those internal triggers like feelings of loneliness and jealousy. Building resilience and directing my attention to digital wellness are more manageable and accessible. Tech is becoming an extension of ourselves, and just like our physical well-being needs attention to get stronger, there are ways to improve our digital wellness muscle.

Earlier in this section, I wrote, "The story I'm telling myself is . . ."

What story are you telling yourself when you reach for your phone or go on social media thirty times a day?

The next time you reach for your phone or spend over an hour on your computer, check in with your greater why. Does it align with how you choose to feel, both physically, mentally, and emotionally? Why are you doing it? What are you getting out of looking at your screen? Build a relationship of awareness with the screens around you and the energy you have within you, and digital wellness will follow. You create your story, written in the actions of this moment.

Cacao, the Heart Opener

I have a dear friend, Angela, who is also my workout buddy, business collaborator, and a boost of joy when I need it. She is a badass, runs her own business, Simplify Home Organizing, and is a Functional health and Happiness Coach. She and I also have a women's circle we started two years ago called "Woman Creating Abundance." About six women get together monthly to support and empower each other with their business ventures. It was surprising when Angela told me she thinks she has a problem, an addiction, to social media.

One Saturday, I went over to her house to prepare ceremonial-grade cacao for a cacao (pure chocolate) ceremony and yoga event we were doing that evening for a yoga retreat I was hosting in town. Cacao is a plant medicine, which is not the same as milk chocolate or even dark chocolate from the store. We don't get a bunch of dark chocolate bars and melt them. This cacao is sourced from a friend, Mat, who moved to Guatemala, started a cacao business, and helped the Indigenous people there while creating a remarkable product. They use pure chocolate beans from the tree to toast and mold into blocks to sell. My family and I went to Guatemala to see where Mat lives, near Lake Atitlán, and immerse ourselves in the unconventional life of a cacao business owner. I bought this cacao from Holy Wow Cacao, knowing it came from a pure source, where each person in the process was treated with love.

That Saturday, when I visited Angela, it felt like a dream to be able to drop my son off at his grandparent's house and go over to my friend's to prepare for this special event. Soon, her kitchen was under the spell of chocolate magic. Working with this heart medicine helps people open up, and I was curious to hear more about her difficulty with social media. We stood in her kitchen, preparing the space to slice the blocks of cacao. We each had our station with a cutting board, knife, and cacao block.

After a few minutes of figuring out the proper measurements for the sixteen people we were serving, I asked her about her social media use. "I spend too much time on my phone, not just social media. It's everything. Part of it is because I have an aversion to using my computer because of twelve years of sitting at a desk for eight hours a day, feeling chained to my desk in front of a screen." I knew the feeling from college, the internship I did to graduate, and the jobs I had with excess computer work. The average American spends seven hours and four minutes looking at a screen every day, according to the Data Reportal in 2022 (Moody 2022).

As we chopped the block of Cacao, she continued to share. "I have realized that I go to my phone when I avoid a task or seek connection. Mostly, I go to Facebook or Facebook Messenger. I watched something that said the original designers didn't realize what they were doing and the impact on everyone's behavior and psyche." A silence swept the kitchen, and I saw her still processing what she was going to say. "I do it when I'm lonely or having a depressing day. Sometimes I do find that connection I'm seeking from Facebook Messenger. And I've tried a bunch of things already, from downloading an app about a year ago that tells me how much I'm on my phone, and it didn't change my behavior. Then on my phone, it has something called digital well-being, where I've set a bunch of cool things, like automatically going to 'do not disturb' and dimming the screen. I also have a calm app that tells me,

'Time to start winding down for bed, Angela!' and I'm like, 'Thanks, Calm App.'"

I'd finished chopping my block, so I stood near the kitchen counter, listening to her as she continued to explain her tech habits as she finished cutting her block. My hands were covered with brown chocolate powder. I let it sit on my hands while she talked. "I notice I will be doing work and focus, and then I will pick up my phone at certain times of the day, for no reason, a lot!"

I asked, "When you spend too long on your phone, how do you feel?"

"Terrible." She responded almost instantly. "I feel depressed, tired, sad, stiff, and icky. My happiest days are the days when I spend less time on my phone consistently. And I notice that I am more present with who I am with, what I am doing, and I don't have to look at my phone."

When she said all of these things, I silently screamed, "Me too!"

I asked Angela, "What does connection mean to you?"

"Mmm, great question." I anticipated her having a definition memorized, but she took a minute to respond, repeating the word aloud a few times. "Connection is a sense of belonging, intimacy with others, myself, higher power, Spirit, the Universe, God, whatever. I have to ponder that more. I have never thought about that. And sometimes, I genuinely feel it when I see heartfelt posts on social media about friends having babies or getting a promotion, or 'I am struggling with X.' Other times, I get off and feel a little more depressed and lonelier. For example, if I see people with others, sometimes that triggers more loneliness and increases my longing for connection."

I listened intently to what she was saying, which voiced an observation that rings true for so many people. If you aren't one of them, you might know someone with that same pattern when on social media. We heated the water, added the cacao and spices, and kept it brewing on the stove until everything melted together; we wove in our blessed intentions for that evening. Our time preparing the cacao felt like a real connection.

Attention Economy

Just for a moment, can I have your undivided attention? What does undivided attention mean in an age when some of you are listening to an audiobook while driving or reading in between the buzzes of Snapchat and text messages? It is important not to blame yourself, and you are not the one at fault here for the tech habits you have created. Intelligent forces are conspiring to manipulate our attention to benefit their company's profits swiftly.

Apps and big tech companies purposely create different ways to exploit our attention. Former Google Design Ethicist Tristan Harris describes our phones as slot machines, offering irregular rewards to hijack our attention and desires (2016). This results from the "attention economy," an internet shaped around advertising to maximize page views, effectively turning our attention into an item to buy and sell (Harris 2016).

Your attention is scarce, and tech companies do everything they can to keep you hooked so you spend more time online, which means more money for them. We want to believe companies like Google and Instagram want the best outcome for humanity, but what happens when our existence runs on an algorithm? They are not only using psychology to keep us on these devices but they are using it to predict our following behavior. You may agree that there is something seriously wrong with this.

After admitting we are not the problem, we can build our self-control and take little actions. For example, turn off our notifications, put our phone somewhere else at night, or use some other methods described in this book to feel more connected with life and less reliant on our devices to dictate where our focus goes.

Since I spoke with Angela, she created space for not using her phone during her day. For example, she does not have her phone at the gym. She set boundaries with her device when she needed more self-care. She also entered a relationship that gave her more human connection, which she was craving. It is inspiring to see her shift her awareness of her habits and reflect on how technology affects her. Because of that, she is changing her relationship with technology to foster more connection in her life, which feeds her soul with the connection we all long for.

Digital Detox

It is common not to find the connection we long for on our phones, but how can we know that when we have them on us all the time? "Digital Detox" is a term that refers to disconnecting from digital devices in order to reconnect with life. It is a practice I partake in at least once a week for a short time, and at least once a year for at least three to five days. Personally, I love the accountability of a friend doing it with me. I offer guided Digital Detox and personal coaching to provide accountability and motivation because it can be tough! There are various ways to do it, and before you breakup with your phone and computer for a day or week, it's important to discover your *why*. Is it to sleep better? For deeper connection? To break a social media addiction? Reduce stress? Or any of the other reasons inspired by this book?

Next, choose how you will do a tech cleanse and visualize what it will look like for you. Here are some examples:

Once a Week:

- Place your phone on airplane mode; only use it for required alarms, calendars, voice recordings, etc. You can use your computer for work or school-related activities. Don't use it for music, texts, calls, or social media.

- Go without using your cell phone. Turn it completely off and place it in one designated spot for the day. Post a sticky note on it with a reminder that it is okay. For instance, "Relax. What's really bothering you? How can you solve this without a phone or let it go?"

- Go without all technology, including a phone, computer, watch, television, and other digital devices. For one day, turn them off, occupy your time with friends, study, read a real book, do yoga, exercise, journal, or spend time in nature.

For One Week:

- Disconnect from social media including Snapchat, Facebook, Instagram, and other social networks.

- Disconnect from the television and things you may watch on TV or Netflix that may be "time wasters." This includes looking up news, following a show online, and other forms of media access. Spend this time doing the things that feed your soul.

- Take a tech cleanse from all devices. This includes email, smartphone use, television, and other electronic devices you use daily. Only use tech for absolutely necessary tasks. For example, for finding directions, working, or doing school-related tasks. You can try to use tech for thirty minutes a day to see how the reduced time feels.

To unplug from something you are so accustomed to in your daily life, you might ask yourself: What will I do with this time? How will I connect with my friends? How will I feel safe? How can I understand myself better?

Here are general guidelines to help you create the most effective use of your energy and time during a technology cleanse. Tech cleanses are most effective if you do them for two or more days. The more time you allocate to this, the more you will get out of it.

Preparation:

- Choose a day that you will start and end. Then, commit to a specific tech cleanse that will work for you. This may be different each time you partake in a temporary breakup from your devices. Be adaptable each time you begin a new one.

- Solidify plans with friends you have that day or week.

- Before the day or week of the cleanse, get all work or schoolwork done you'd need a computer or phone for. A prime time for a long tech cleanse is after finals or before a new job.

- Let family, friends, coworkers, professors, boss, mentors, or any other people present in your weekly life know you are doing a tech cleanse and what to expect during the time you do it. The amount of detail you share is up to you. I encourage you to be clear with your partner or close friends on how you can be reached and to clearly communicate any needs that need to be met. This gives a sense of peace and trust.

- Set an automated email for work or friends, saying you will be away from the computer and phone and why.

- Look at your "5 things that bring you joy" list from Tech Step 5 and choose one or two to do during this time. Plan a fun, creative day without technology. For example: go on a picnic, read a book, connect with people you don't know, start a creative project, read, play music, paint, play a sport, or travel. Write down these plans and give them up to a higher power to lead the way. Another option is to not plan ANYTHING! So much of what we do is planned, and we adhere to a schedule. This may be that day when you let all of that go and have absolutely no plan. An unplanned day allows you to trust in your intuition and what the universe will bring to you that day.

- Make time for self-reflection, creativity, meditation, and/or yoga. These activities will help you reflect and gain a new outlook on adulting and acceptance for who you are today.

During:

Remember, fear is normal, especially during the first twenty-four hours. It will feel like something is missing, like you are not safe, like you are alone. Be with the fears that arise, feel them, and release them when the time feels right. Each time you do a Digital Detox, the fear will transform more to love, presence, and connection. Take a deep breath, relax. You are completely capable of doing this.

The one thing that will help process this time, I've discovered, is not releasing all that is buried inside you to a friend, unless that friend is a willing, trained therapist or counselor. What helps is journaling. Actual handwriting, not typing on a device. This method is encouraged because handwriting can help you comprehend and recall information better than typing. Another tool for expression is painting. Do something with your hands that helps you slow down. Each time I do a Digital Detox, I fill up at least five pages in my journal. I encourage you to share your emotions, any signs or signals you receive, physical or mental blocks you are working through, or situations in life you are seeking clarity on.

A tech cleanse gives you the ability to cultivate a sense of patience and contemplate small and large decisions that affect your life. Part of spiritual growth is the application of all the lessons you are given. By taking a break from tech, the knowledge and lessons turn into wisdom. This wisdom becomes a part of you and a part of how you can contribute to the world. Take time to contemplate decisions that matter in your life. It is valuable to spend time with yourself without distractions and to get to know your inner child and your true self.

After:

Before you turn on your phone or sign in to your social media platforms, notice how you are feeling. Are you disgusted? Overwhelmed? Joyful? Excited? Fully feel that emotion and investigate why you may be feeling that way. Take note of that feeling as you move forward. Have an intentional moment to turn on your devices with awareness. Thank tech for all it does in your life and use it with more purpose.

After the cleanse, you may go back to your screen habits. Although the action of doing so will be the same, you will be different. There will be a shift. Out of the whole process, this is one of the most important parts of the tech cleanse. Not because you are using your phone again (Woo-hoo! or maybe Oh sh*t!), but because over the past day or week, you've created an extremely valuable awareness of yourself. You've built trust with yourself. You've truly honored your existence by allowing yourself to come back to the truth of what you are experiencing in your life. Recognizing this takes integrity, vulnerability, and spiritual courage.

Tech Step 9: Digital Wellness Diet

If a Digital Detox doesn't fit into your life currently, it's okay. There are other options that can help create more time connecting with others and bring healthy habits of technology use into your life. Since the pandemic, you may spend more time on screens than on actual in-person connections. Are you wanting more in-person connections but don't know how to begin tackling the elephant in the room—your digital habits?

Some of our habits involve daily doses of social media, news, or communication. You may indulge, or overindulge, in a nice treat of Instagram while you have your morning coffee. According to a survey by the International Data Corporation (IDC), of 7,446 individuals between eighteen and forty-four years old, 79 percent reach for their phone first thing when they wake up (2013).

Based on where you are with your phone and social media use, answer the questions below that reflect where your energy is going and where it is leaking.

Step 1: Reflect on where your energy is going in the morning and evening.

Step 2: Write down what you do each morning and night. Reflect on these routines that you've developed. Be honest with yourself without trying to change anything.

Step 3: Within these morning and evening hours of the day, how do you lead by example when using a screen with presence?

Step 4: What would it feel like if you were to disconnect or unplug for thirty minutes or a few hours in your morning or evening? What would it look like for you?

Step 5: What ways can you replace screen time with an activity that feeds your soul? Example: Reflecting on my day in the evening with my partner instead of watching TV.

Review your answers and prepare to make one change to your daily routine. This does not have to be an extravagant change but one that is manageable and can help you create a deeper relationship with yourself. Digital wellness doesn't have to be challenging, but it can change your life.

Chapter Ten

An Entrepreneur's Heart

When I got back from Israel, I had no job, and I moved back in with my parents in Orlando, Florida. The same house, yet a completely changed me. I relied on them as I figured out my motive and motion toward a career. It was a juncture in time filled with unknowns. It wasn't long before I found a Kundalini Yoga Center in Orlando. I went on the day of the Kundalini Yoga Teacher Training. During the relaxation, I lay there feeling at home in my heart. After the class, I asked one of the training coordinators how far along they were in their training. Surprisingly, they were only a few weeks ahead of the teacher training I left in Israel. I planned on returning to

Israel a few months later if the cash magically appeared for me to go. I had deep gratitude when they told me I could join and finish training in Orlando instead of traveling back to Israel.

As I continued the training, I looked for jobs and practiced yoga. Occasionally, I'd get caught up in what other people were doing with the snippets of their lives after college they posted online. I saw people I knew going to grad school, moving across the country, finding their dream job, marrying the love of their life, and I was living with my parents with no job, completing my second yoga teacher training. I didn't have many friends I connected with where my parents lived, and I would get in my head. I'd overanalyze, criticize, and be hard on myself. Then, I'd do things that brought me back into balance, like play tennis or hang out with the two friends I did have. Still, there were so many unknowns that my mind was trying to figure out every little detail.

My mental health was suffering. When I surrendered the anxiety and worry and understood that this was only my mind's defense mechanism, opportunities came to me.

One week, I visited where I went to school, Gainesville, Florida, hoping to move back there. On a hot Florida evening, I went to the farmer's market and saw a friend named Michael. He was in the Krishna Consciousness Movement when I met him and cooked terrific vegetarian food. We spoke for a little while over the band playing and people scooting passed us to get their vegetables. I mentioned my situation in Orlando.

"Woah! I have a room opening up in my house in the next week or so." A glimmer appeared in his eye as if the search to find the perfect roommate was complete. Later that month, I stuffed all my belongings into my car and moved in with Michael, who'd eventually be the person I'd have a child with and build our lives intertwined together.

Still living off my parent's money, I knew I needed to find a job and start my career as a spiritual hippy yogi. Living with this identity, I'd get rich by burning two things: myself out with thirty classes a week and incense. I had multiple jobs because I resisted the forty-hour-a-week desk job working for someone else. There was no way I'd sell my soul to a business where I'd dread going to work. I saw people throughout my life do this, like my mother, for several years.

Instead, I taught yoga at a summer camp and PE for an incredible charter school with a woman principal who inspired me daily. Also, I worked for a nonprofit crypto currency company, yoga studios, and Uber. Some days, teaching PE was energizing for me, and other days, the kids sucked all the energy out of me.

On top of this transition into work, I was responsible for rent, insurance, and the heavy responsibilities of an adult. The transition to adulthood felt rushed, and there were many times I improvised my way. Although my steady yoga practice taught me there was nothing I couldn't handle, I still experienced being in my head more than I was in my heart, which would cause me to struggle with giving and receiving love.

I had patience for myself and surrounded myself with people with similar interests and values. After years of building up a community in the town that I didn't plan on leaving for a while, I felt more and more united with how I lived. It took time to build my confidence to enter the workforce untraditionally. Though I loved what I was doing, the entrepreneurial lifestyle and the cloud of stress that followed me were not realistic for my long-term goals.

Transition

As much as I loved my four jobs, I didn't want to drive drunk fraternity guys around or teach children how to play kickball forever. I did want to develop my love for mind/body medicine and wellness. I was confident I had a calling to help people with their digital health and overall well-being. This calling would not stop knocking at my door.

I decided to put more energy into that part of my life. I taught more workshops, did more presentations at the University of Florida, and continued to pour my heart into those things that energized and uplifted my spirit. I didn't spend as much time looking at what other people were doing online. Instead, I paid more attention to what I was doing to improve my health and well-being. I went on walks, spent more time making and maintaining healthy friendships, exercised, and voiced my boundaries toward things that would not support my growth. I directed my energy toward building skills and strengths I was inherently good at and loved to do, including teaching and leading events. Although yoga wouldn't pay all my bills, it was a time of deep trust that I was exactly where I needed to be.

Little did I know that this transition into adulting would help me build resilience for all the other shifts I'd go through in my twenties. When I was on the cusp of giving up on my dreams, a universal sign or message would appear right before me, like when I saw Michael at the farmer's market. If not addressed, the struggle and stress in adulthood are real and affect our long-term mental health. According to Johns Hopkins Medicine (2022), one in four adults who are eighteen and older are diagnosed with a mental health disorder, and many take prescription medications. One in six of these adults takes a psychiatric drug (Johns Hopkins Medicine 2022).

Severe life events, including the transition from college to adulthood, trigger many people who struggle with mental illness. When there is consciousness around this adulting process, you can honestly sit with yourself, ask what you need, and follow through with the guidance you receive.

Inevitably, life will bring challenges, spiritual tests, and moments of extreme discomfort. What shapes your experiences is your response to those moments; usually, it isn't in the moment that you decide that. Through meditation and yoga, we develop the resilience to overcome those confounding circumstances when they arise, instead of hiding behind our phones, hoping they will save us. Life is about constantly growing in various ways. My attempt at being an entrepreneur brought me to many places that appeared to be dead ends at first but were an opportunity for me to climb over the mountain and sometimes dance up the hill.

The New "Unconventional" Norm

The COVID-19 pandemic affected many of us, causing us to reevaluate our life direction. In 2021, the nation's quit rate was at an all-time high. While many people quit their careers of choice, I surrendered to opportunities to grow professionally. I got my first full-time job during this worldly crisis. After spending the first four years after school figuring out who I was, I prayed for something that supported my growth as a professional and financially stable, conscious adult.

It all changed when my boobs started getting bigger, and I saw the positive sign on my first pregnancy test. "This is my calling, being a stay-at-home mother," I thought.

It turns out that changing poopy diapers three to five times a day and talking to an infant was more complicated than it seemed. It is some mothers' life's purpose, but it was not my dream path. After a year of watching my incredible son grow and develop, a tremendous blessing, I needed something more to contribute to my community. Before I could do that, I had to surrender a belief holding me back: the entrepreneurial idea that a full-time job had to be some horrible experience in a toxic environment, acting like a robot for a whole day.

This old story came from seeing people sitting miserably at a computer all day. Other influences, like no freedom or flexibility with a full-time job, molded this belief. These beliefs were no longer beneficial for where life was taking me.

I worked on this belief until it was completely erased and replaced with a truth aligned with me. I changed my story and created a new one that aligned with my spirit. I decided that any job I choose to manifest will be a job I love, and for a company whose values align with mine. I will choose to serve out of love instead of fear. Within months of visualizing the ideal job, a job opened as a group fitness manager at Gainesville Health and Fitness, a well-known US health club, where I taught yoga a few times a week.

As soon as I saw the job posting, something in me knew I had the job. After three diligent weeks of interviews, something I was out of practice with, I received the joyful news that I got the position. I requested a stand-up desk, set up my hippie crystals around my computer monitor, and started on my way to learning a different way of being in the workforce.

The first year in my full-time position had everything I wanted in a first job: innovation, independence, steadiness, and helping people. After that year, I missed those precious moments I had at home with my son and family. I started working on weekends to keep up with the demands of managing eighty teachers, and I found myself dissatisfied with the pay I received, barely enough to afford our newly bought house. I gradually went back to old habits of filling my schedule with more and more work and still feeling like I didn't have enough money or satisfaction in my life.

I taught kids tennis, got my real estate license, and started a workplace wellness business, Oracle Wellness, LLC. It was nearly impossible to remove all the heavy hats on my head. In addition, I'd see my son for about two hours every workday. I felt like I was cheating as a mother and neglecting to mother myself. I'd take my lunch break to walk around a trail barefoot near my work and escape the fluorescent lights and stimulation.

Then there was that moment. That moment when burnout wet my face with tears and my mental health dripped to the floor. I felt helpless and scared. It wasn't the type of hit that happens in one moment, but it was a buildup of all the pressure I'd put on myself over the past few years. I permitted myself to glimpse through the eyes of my consciousness and hear what She was trying to say. What she was saying was not what my logical brain wanted to hear. I felt stuck in doubt and fear and like running from everything, my natural tendency when things got hard. Instead of doing that, which my young entrepreneur-ey self would have done, I decided to ride the wave and see where it led me.

Human Touch

Do you remember a time in your life when the steps you took felt like they weren't your own? Maybe they were your parent's steps, the steps of your culture, or the steps of the story you built up in your mind of what you were supposed to be. When we enter the workforce as young adults, there are many detours on our authentic path. There is no shame in starting over again and again, because that third time you start over, you begin from a space of experience.

When I first owned a business, while working another full-time job, I felt more confident in my abilities than ever. The parts of me that were passionate about what I was doing still lived within me, and now I had the experience to back me up. I saw a vision, and I recognized it would take longer than a year to accomplish all my soul longed for. As the years passed, my vision expanded into the long-term manifestations of my life. I trusted in myself and knew what I needed to build back up in times of stress.

For once in my life, the instant gratification I grew up around was no longer my motivation. It was my resounding *why*. My why manifested in boundaries and clear intentions. On countless Saturdays, I turned off my phone and left it at home while traveling to the beach. I silenced notifications and plunged into one conversation and project at a time. The connections I created with others were something that automation can never replace.

More and more, we see different automated jobs. For example, you rarely speak with a natural person when you chat on any website with an instant messenger. Automation is all around us and only increasing. A friend of mine, Harmony, was recently doing her internship for nursing school in a Neuro ICU. She mentioned the nurse rolled around an AI interface with a TV of the doctor's face. The doctor was not on the hospital premises or readily available if he was needed in person. Harmony explained that it was efficient, yet there was a loss of connection from patient to doctor and nurse to doctor.

Artificial intelligence, machine learning, robotics, and other fields where they are developing technology to replace jobs are inevitable in the workforce. Occasionally, I feel depressed knowing humans can be replaced with robots in many crucial positions. But there will never be another you. Being aware of how these machines are integrating themselves into the workplace is something to be mindful of but not something that can ever replace your existence on this planet. You can be an advocate for ethical and moral technology and continue to serve in a way that aligns with your values. Human touch is needed; the further we get away from human and spirit connection, the more people will crave personal contact with others.

Conscious Adulting is not some carved-out roadmap, but there are tools to help you get there. You can locate many of these tools with your wise internal compass, though you may unveil some through conversation, nature, or those tiny moments that light you up. Digital wellness holds many keys that can open the locks to our overall well-being. With the overwhelming amount of responsibility, career choices, family dynamics, and more, occasionally, we need a break from making the choices to reset our vision and remember why.

Tech Step 10: Choice Fatigue

How often have you thought of fantastic possibilities of the direction of your life and ended up feeling overwhelmed with all the options and ultimately chose none? What about saying you will complete your to-do list for the day, but you get distracted by many small demands of life or a show that keeps you hooked? There are so many choices available, and some preoccupy your attention with what you are truly craving.

Sometimes I feel burnt out from making so many choices that I neglect my essential ability to care for myself. What am I going to eat for dinner that evening? When do I need to go to bed? We make thousands of decisions per day in our real life, and those decisions shape our reality. In addition, we make thousands of decisions in our digital life.

When becoming adults, we are often overwhelmed by these big and small decisions that can impact us for years, from deciding to take a full-time job to starting your own business. The decision to have children or to wait. The decision to spend that money you were saving or invest it. What if there was a way to create more stability and simplicity within our decision-making system? How can these ways offer a better understanding of who we are? These three tech steps have worked for me and others who own or manage businesses. In some way, we are all managers of our own life, and as a leader, may you feel empowered in (mostly) all your decisions.

1. Energy Enhancer - Energy enhancer is our ability to create, sustain, and elevate our energy. When we can consolidate our power, we can better direct this toward tasks of meaning. You have the capacity to connect with this vibrancy as an energy budget, because we all love budgeting, right? Take inventory of where you spend your daily physical, mental, digital, and emotional energy. Sometimes, being aware of your vibrancy is enough to change how you spend it.

2. Mood Elevator - Our moods and emotions are constantly changing, as it is part of human nature to experience the ebb and flow of these natural states. For some, we have more awareness and control over our emotions, while others allow their feelings to control them. Yoga and meditation are proven techniques to regulate your limbic system, the emotional center of your brain. We can regulate our emotional reactions to situations and respond with more awareness. When we make decisions, there is a certain level of grief. We grieve the possibility of that other option and the person who could have chosen that. What are your tactics to self-regulate when you feel overwhelmed with grief, anger, sadness, or joy? Do you healthfully express or go for the pizza?

3. Seek Serenity - Our lives are bombarded with distraction, distortion, illusion, and clutter. Serenity is not necessarily easy to find in this world of chaos unless you actively seek it. Creating a spiritual practice or connection to nature can help you prepare to use the daily decision-making power you inherently have. Serenity is also found in small moments, like a hug or a cuddle with your pet.

Divine power awaits you when you open the door to peace and allow it to hold space in your routine.

As a Conscious Adult, you control your energy, choices, and decisions. Buddha states, "Change is never painful, only resistance to change is painful."

Chapter Eleven

The Impact

When technology rapidly advanced when I was a child, parents did their best to understand what this meant for children. Tech came in at a time when our collective immune system was down. As a culture, we were already eating junk food, losing sleep, and disconnecting from our health and well-being. In many instances, tech was given to children, no matter what age, with no contemplation about the consequences. I was one of those children who had very little supervision with its many functions. I wasn't into anything inappropriate besides the occasional prank phone call or R-rated internet exploration with friends. The internet gives children, and anyone for that matter, freedom their brains and consciousness are not ready to absorb.

I don't blame my parents for giving me these stylish devices, and I don't blame myself for the unknowing consequences I exhibited later in life, like retraining my brain to focus on one book at a time. It was the thing to do, the tech fad. It's still the fad to have the latest technology on your lap, even during a meaningful conversation. Studies show that more devices and more time on these gadgets aren't necessarily better. It's like the diet scientists proving junk food makes you more overweight. Though there are some benefits to those feel-good foods, there is more compelling evidence to prove it decreases our overall health.

It is not too late to create awareness and change. You are the difference through your story, applied Tech Steps, and healthy relationship with screens. From there, we can teach our youth what we may not have been given as a child but learned later. We have the answers, not at our fingertips from our devices, but from the present interaction, play, and experience that come from childhood. The social, emotional, physical, and cognitive development that happens as a child cannot be replaced, even with a screen.

How do we expect our generation and future generations to evolve to their full potential when instantly gratified by a screen?

As a woman who grew up in the evolving digital atmosphere, I can confidently say there is hope for the millennial generation, Gen Z, Gen A, and our future generations. Hope lies within the small, subtle moments of your awareness and exchange with the world. A hope that doesn't leave us in disbelief that technology is ruining our children but instead challenges these fads we've come to know as normal. A hope that empowers me to be the light that shines brighter than the attractive blue light emitted from our phones. It is a hope that is so strong, vibrant, and present that it leaves no choice but to disconnect and reconnect to consciousness.

Small Moments

I went through ebbs and flows with attachments to my device. Through these, I'd attempt to leave my phone when

I knew I didn't need it and cleanse from this dependence at least three times a year.

I purposely left my phone at home one morning while going to the farmer's market. I figured I'd be present with my son, which is the most important thing for me to do. That mild anxiety of leaving my phone at home hit me when I went to look for it as we approached the market.

After I remembered I had left it at home, my anxiety faded as I noticed the smiling faces surrounding the honey stand. I looked back at my son strapped in his car seat and was back in the feeling of joy and connection to him. I sat him in his stroller and walked casually around the farmer's market, saying hello to familiar faces that I may not have noticed if my phone had been on me. After selecting fresh greens, I handed the wrinkled farmer my card. He used his phone to charge me six dollars. We saw people taking photos with their iPhones, beautiful show-quality dogs, and a man strumming his guitar to a song he had written. My son got out of his stroller, started dancing, and asked me to join him. We laughed together as we held hands, spinning around between the crowd shuffling past. Julian and I felt the energy of being in a place filled with fresh food and good energy. It felt like being alive.

For that moment at the farmer's market, I didn't want to worry about time, unimportant notifications, or capturing the moment. I was present with my child, and that gave my life meaning. In addition, there wasn't a feeling of *fuck technology. I'm better than those people.* I experienced gratitude for my ability to pay for my food and the countless devices it took to create the market I was standing in.

As we continued to walk past the goods booths, Julian saw something that caught his eye. "Mama!" His eyes widened, and he lifted his hand to point at a large cage over ten feet away.

"Wow! That is a goat. Let's go over there and see it." As excited as he was, I felt just as excited, and this childlike curiosity overtook me. We strolled past people carrying bags of vegetables to get to a baby goat at a stand that sold goat products. I unstrapped Julian so he could get an up-close look at the goat's wire-looking fur. Two sisters around the age of five pouted as their mom directed them to stand in a specific way to get a photo of them in front of the goat.

"No, Mom! I just want to pet it. I don't want a picture."

The mom fiercely ran around the cage, snapping pictures from all angles, then led them toward another stand as we walked closer. We got up to the goat, and I crouched to his level. Instead of filling up my camera roll, I was filled with amusement to experience this moment with Julian, both in awe of the wondrous creature. Although he may not remember this specific instance, it is these moments that weave together our life, and it's these moments we can choose to be fully present with or tend to never fully live because of our phones, watches, and other devices.

Parenting Yourself

I think about the world Julian is growing up in frequently. Along with the abundance of other issues his generation will overcome, technology is one of those topics that will seep into his existence.

I ask myself questions: How will he balance the time and energy spent online versus in person? Will he be addicted to video games or other forms of entertainment? Will technology manipulate his attention even more than it did with my generation? What can I do right now to help him learn to use technology consciously? Children are given an immense amount of responsibility when they are handed a device. A child or teenager growing up in the digital age has a hard time thinking about the consequences of looking up, say, porn. Or spending hours gaming and less time on in-person connection. Every family dynamic looks different, and giving a child a phone absolutely has its benefits, such as engagement with peers and contact with parents. It is important to develop a household with screen-time etiquette to pass on to our children. As parents, we are their first teachers.

My partner, Michael, and I have very similar views on parenting and screens. When I met Michael, he still had a flip phone when the latest iPhone came out in 2017. The more we researched technology and children, the more we decided against some common uses of technology with children. We choose this because the science shows how it affects sleep, attention and focus, violence and aggressive behaviors, and learning and development.

We looked at studies from the National Institutes of Health, including the Adolescent Brain Cognitive

Development (ABCD) study, which cited children who reported more than two hours a day of screen time got lower scores on thinking and language tests (Paulich et al. 2021). Children are sleeping less, have a lower attention span, are more obese, and have fewer social skills than before the prevalence of technology (Paulich et al. 2021).

For me to enforce these behaviors with Julian meant that Michael and I chose to be highly aware of our screen habits before we even decided to have children. We love to take cute baby photos and watch a show occasionally. Yet we don't own a television, and we have a charging station where our phones live most of the time we are home. These boundaries shape how we hold the space for our child's development and our connection to each other. We are on devices around Julian with awareness, and for valid reasons, not usually to scroll social media. Our child knows us as parents that pay attention to his needs; not ones that are constantly on our phones. Those precious memories at the farmer's market, playing in the dirt, getting messy with pizza dough, and going on a scooter walk outweigh the times we connect to our devices.

You will never see us hand our phones to him at the dinner table or in the car. As parents, we've consciously chosen to expose him, but not immerse him, in screens. To share this is to show you it is possible to live without devices at the center. Each household is different and can decide how they choose to integrate devices into their families. Just like you witnessed your parent's relationship with screens, children are watching and soaking it in like a sponge.

Yes, there are the grandparents who allow more screen time than I ever do. I do my best to give Julian the space to make his own choices and explore his curiosity. He'll sit next to my dad and watch the lengthy advertisements with basketball in between. He will engage with a show at my in-law's house. There are opportunities for him to see other children playing on their tablets or learning from an educational program.

There is no GPS or roadmap for parenting, and it is one of life's most significant responsibilities. While a child's brain rapidly develops in the first years, a parent guides their soul, leading by example. What if you allowed yourself two or three hours to play? Explore your childlike curiosity. Let your mind wander and your inner child be free. What does it feel like when you can be the mother to yourself that you've always needed?

Tech Step 11: Role Model

Almost every day, I see a child sitting in a stroller with an iPhone or at a restaurant with an iPad, or the parent is on their phone while feeding their baby. These are everyday situations in this tech age. I don't judge, because who am I to look at someone and know their story? I don't.

What isn't so common is someone like you stepping out of that norm to facilitate a connection with the real world, especially when in the presence of children.

Duration: 3–10 minutes

Step 1: In a quiet space, close your eyes and imagine yourself in the presence of a child. How are you going to show your full attention to this kid? What technology boundaries will you set to lead this child you are fully present with?

This child can be you or a child you know and love. Children crave attention, just like you do. By doing this, you are helping this kid, and yourself, create a deeper connection. You have a key to help others unlock their treasure chest of attention. Express your creativity and be fearlessly authentic as you interact with the world with your full engagement. You are worthy of being fully conscious as an adult in the digital age.

The Journey Home

In this chapter of your life, where you set the foundation for each step you take, you are doing it with more awareness by opening the pages of this book and opening your heart to possibilities. This path of conscious adulting is meant to be celebrated along the way. If you have made it to the end of this book, completing most of the exercises (let's be real, you likely didn't do all of them), then that is worthy of celebrating. How do you celebrate with awareness and joy? I, for one, love to have friends over to drink Cacao and share a meal.

If you choose not to celebrate because this is only another book on the nightstand that you pop open to read every once in a while, may you be reminded that you are worthy of being celebrated daily. You are worthy of all the miracles that arrive when you look up from your phone and see a hummingbird dancing around a purple flower. You are worthy of a deep connection to yourself, to others, and to life. You are worthy of all the exquisiteness that surrounds you each second of this day.

Congratulations on completing this book and diving into the journey of conscious adulting in the digital age. This is a continuous process of resilience, remembering who you are, and reprogramming your mind and body to live in alignment with your true nature. We have seen how technology can impact our physical, mental, emotional, social, spiritual, and environmental aspects of health if it's not managed in a way that aligns with your goals and values. As I have mentioned in this book, technology has its place in our lives. Using screens with awareness and presence can enhance our life experience instead of impeding our growth.

This journey in Life University is no straight road with a flashing sign saying, "This is the only way." It will have bumps, detours, and mountains to ascent. Yet you will now be connected to your internal compass, so when you lose cellular service, you will continue to trust and stay linked to a higher you. While traveling on your path, look up from your devices and see the blessings surrounding you. Raise yourself above the blocks and ties that are holding you down. Elevate yourself, and in turn, you will uplift others. Be courageous in the pursuit of your journey home.

Reference List

Blankson, Amy, and Nina Hersher. 2021. *Digital Wellness: Your Playbook for Thriving in the Remote Work Era.* Hoboken, NJ: Wiley Beyond and the Digital Wellness Institute. https://universityservices.wiley.com/wp-content/uploads/2021/01/2021-DigitalWellness-eBook.pdf.

Cheng, Cecilia, and Angel Yee-lam Li. 2014. "Internet Addiction Prevalence and Quality of (Real) Life: A Meta-Analysis of 31 Nations Across Seven World Regions." *Cyberpsychology, Behavior, and Social Networking* 17 (12): 755–760. https://doi.org/10.1089/cyber.2014.0317

Dailey, Hannah. 2022. "Selena Gomez Reveals She Hasn't Used the Internet in 4 Years: 'It Makes Me Feel Normal.'" *Billboard*, April 5, 2022. https://www.billboard.com/music/music-news/selena-gomez-no-internet-four-years-1235055475/.

Daniels, Michael. 2021. *Shadow, Self, Spirit: Essays in Transpersonal Psychology*. Exeter: Imprint Academic.

Digital Wellness Institute. n.d. "Digital Wellness Institute." Accessed June 20, 2022. https://www.digitalwellnessinstitute.com/home.

Eating for the Ecosystem Applied Research and Education. 2020. "Nature & The Nervous System." Last modified March 3, 2020. https://efte-are.org/nature-the-nervous-system/.

Eyal, Nir, and Julie Li-Eyal. 2020. *Indistractable: How to Control Your Attention and Choose Your Life*. London: Bloomsbury Publishing.

Franco, L., Shanahan, D. and Fuller, R., 2017. A Review of the Benefits of Nature Experiences: More Than Meets the Eye. *International Journal of Environmental Research and Public Health*, 14(8), p.864.

Gazzaley, Adam, and Larry D. Rosen. 2016. *The Distracted Mind: Ancient Brains in a High-Tech World*. Boston: MIT Press.

Harris, Tristan. 2016. "How Technology Hijacks People's Minds—From a Magician and Google's Design Ethicist." *Observer*, June 1, 2016. https://observer.com/2016/06/how-technology-hijacks-peoples-minds%E2%80%8A-%E2%80%8Afrom-a-magician-and-googles-design-ethicist/.

Hilliard, Jena. 2022. "Social Media Addiction." Last modified May 4, 2022. https://www.addictioncenter.com/drugs/social-media-addiction/.

Hunt, Melissa G., Rachel Marx, Courtney Lipson, and Jordyn Young. 2018. "No More FOMO: Limiting Social Media Decreases Loneliness and Depression." *Journal of Social and Clinical Psychology* 37, no. 10 (December). https://doi.org/10.1521/jscp.2018.37.10.751.

International Data Corporation. 2013. *Always Connected: How Smartphones and Social Keep Us Engaged.* IDC Research Report, Sponsored by Facebook. https://www.nu.nl/files/IDC-Facebook%20Always%20Connected%20(1).pdf.

Johns Hopkins Medicine. 2022. "Mental Health Disorder
    Statistics." Wellness & Prevention. Accessed June
    20, 2022.
    https://www.hopkinsmedicine.org/health/wellness-
    and-prevention/mental-health-disorder-statistics.

Mastroianni, Brian. 2016. "How Generation Z Is Changing
    the Tech World." CBS News. CBS Interactive.
    Accessed April 2, 2022.
    https://www.cbsnews.com/news/social-media-fuels-
    a-change-in-generations-with-the-rise-of-gen-z/.

Moody, Rebecca. 2022. "Screen Time Statistics: Average
    Screen Time in US vs. the rest of the world."
    Comparitech. Last modified March 21, 2022.
    https://www.comparitech.com/tv-streaming/screen-
    time-statistics/.

Morley, Christopher. 2020. Where the Blue Begins. New
    York: Bibliotech Press.

NAMI California. n.d. "Mental Health Benefits of Nature."
    Blog. Accessed June 20, 2022.
    https://namica.org/blog/mental-health-benefits-of-
    nature/.

Newport, Cal. 2016. *Deep Work: Rules for Focused Success in a Distracted World.* New York: Grand Central Publishing.

Orlowski-Yang, Jeff, dir. 2020. *The Social Dilemma.* Hollywood, CA: Netflix. https://www.netflix.com/title/81254224?source=imdb.

Oxford Learner's Dictionaries, s.v. "Adulting (n.)." Accessed June 22, 2022. https://www.oxfordlearnersdictionaries.com/us/definition/english/adulting?q=adulting.

Paulich, Katie N., J. Megan Ross, Jeffrey M. Lessem, and John K. Hewitt. 2021. "Screen Time and Early Adolescent Mental Health, Academic, and Social Outcomes in 9- and 10-Year-Old Children: Utilizing the Adolescent Brain Cognitive Development (ABCD) Study." *PLoS One* 16, no. 9 (September). https://doi.org/10.1371/journal.pone.0256591.

Perrin, Andrew, and Sara Atske. "About Three-In-Ten U.S. Adults Say They Are 'Almost Constantly' Online." Pew Research Center. Last modified March 26, 2021. www.pewresearch.org/fact-tank/2021/03/26/about-three-in-ten-u-s-adults-say-they-are-almost-constantly-online/.

Roberts, James A. 2016. Too Much of a Good Thing: Are You Addicted *to Your Smartphone?* Austin, TX: Sentia Publishing Company.

Sullivan, Bob, and Hugh Thompson. 2013. "Brain, Interrupted." *New York Times*, May 3, 2013. https://www.nytimes.com/2013/05/05/opinion/sunday/a-focus-on-distraction.html.

Weissbourd, Richard, Milena Batanova, Virginia Lovison, and Eric Torrres. 2021. *Loneliness in America: How the Pandemic Has Deepened an Epidemic of Loneliness and What We Can Do About It.* Cambridge, MA: Harvard Graduate School of Education, Making Caring Common Project. https://static1.squarespace.com/static/5b7c56e255b02c683659fe43/t/6021776bdd04957c4557c212/1612805995893/Loneliness+in+America+2021_02_08_FINAL.pdf

Western Governors University. 2019. "Impact of Technology on Kids Today (and Tomorrow)." *WGU Washington*. Information Technology. Last modified

October 3, 2019. https://www.wgu.edu/blog/impact-technology-kids-today-tomorrow1910.html#openSubscriberModal.

White, Mathew P., Ian Alcock, James Grellier, Benedict W. Wheeler, Terry Hartig, Sara L. Warber, Angie Bone, Michael H. Depledge, and Lora E. Fleming. 2019. "Spending At Least 120 Minutes a Week in Nature is Associated with Good Health and Wellbeing." *Scientific Reports* 9, 7730. https://doi.org/10.1038/s41598-019-44097-3

Additional Resources

Ayurveda Books

Ayurveda: The Science of Self Healing: A Practical Guide by Vasant Lad

Practical Ayurveda: Find Out Who You Are and What You Need to Bring Balance to Your Life by Sivananda Yoga Vedanta Centre

Ayurveda Beginner's Guide: Essential Ayurvedic Principles and Practices to Balance and Heal Naturally by Susan Weis-Bohlen

Extensions for Internet Browsers

Cold Turkey

FocusMe

Focus App

Phone Apps

To Track Screen Time Habits:

Quality Time

YourHour

MyAddictometer

Help with Time Management and Productivity:

StayFocusd

BlockSite

App Block

Freedom

OFFTIME

Stay on Task (Android)

Moment (iOS)

Apple's Screen Time

Tools to Help with a Digital Detox:

Detox Procrastination Blocker

BreakFree (iOS, Android)

Flipd (iOS, Android)

AppDetox (Android)

About the Author

Melissa Baker (Honey Bee) is a multi-passionate Certified Health Education Specialist, Digital Wellness Coach, and Writer who lives in Gainesville, FL. Along with teaching yoga, meditation, and fitness to kids and adults, she hosts health retreats and corporate wellness initiatives. Her business, Oracle Wellness (Oraclewellness.org), has helped her achieve her vision of bringing wellness to diverse cultures and groups. She is passionate about assisting others to access and connect to their authentic expression of themselves through yoga, meditation, and movement-based therapies, as well as creating harmony with their outer technology. Her vision is to help millions with their Digital Well-being.

After being addicted to screens as a teenager and overwhelmed with it in college, her view drastically shifted after she began to change her screen-time habits. Since then, her awareness of screens, and their effects on various aspects of health, empowered her to change her life and guide others to shift their digital habits to ones that align with their values.